Travels in Tuscany

Fiona and Innes Fennell

MEREHURST PRESS
LONDON

For Terence and Inez

Published 1988 by Merehurst Press
5 Great James Street
London WC1N 3DA

Co-published in Australia and New Zealand by
Child and Associates
5 Skyline Place, French's Forest
Sydney 2086
Australia

ISBN 1 85391 004 X

Printed in Great Britain by Hartnolls Limited

Typeset by Maggie Spooner Typesetting
Designed and produced by Snap! Books
Illustrations by Anne Forrest
Cover illustration by Malcolm Forrest
Maps by Sue Lawes

Contents

Acknowledgements

Our sincere thanks to the many people who have
helped us with this book; Sevenoaks Travel, the
Restaurateurs and Hoteliers who looked after us
so well and our newly found Italian friends who
gave us so much information

Lastly, we would like to say a special thank you
to our great friend, Nicki, whose research and
hard work have proved invaluable.

Preface

After the success of our first book, *Travels in the Dordogne*, Innes and I were delighted to be asked to write more of our travels. Here we have chosen Northern Italy — a fourteen-day holiday in the Tuscany region. Tuscany has a varied landscape, a hot climate and a wealth of history and art, not forgetting its interesting food and wine.

It is therefore, an ideal place for a holiday and I am certain that you will enjoy it as much as we did.

In the pages which follow, you will find a brief historical summary of Italy as a whole, followed by a full introduction to Tuscany. This, we hope, will help you to appreciate the area to the full. The particular places we have chosen for you to visit are our favourites, but are also designed to give you a fair sampling of the variety within Tuscany and thus to awaken your determination to investigate this region of Italy, described by many as the jewel in Italy's crown.

If you are, unfortunately, short of time, then I suggest that you travel from Lucca to Florence one year, and on from Florence to Volterra as soon as you can.

Fiona Fennell

Fomova Lasco

Introduction to Italy

A Turbulent Heritage

Cathedral — Volterra

Italy, as a country, is instantly recognisable on any world map, its boot shaped peninsula jutting out into the Mediterranean. Eighty percent is mountainous: to the north, running west to east, are the Alps and Dolomites which protected Italy from invasion by North European Barbarians during ancient times. The rest of Italy is bordered by the calm waters of the Mediterranean sea which first acted as a route inwards for other civilizations, and later as a highway outwards for the expansion of the Roman Empire. The Apennine range zig-zags down the centre of the country to form Italy's backbone, and is largely volcanic in origin. Thus the plains of Tuscany, Latium and Campania were covered with ash and lava producing the rich fertile farmlands which can be seen today.

Although the home of one of Europe's oldest recorded civilizations, as a country it has only been united since 1870.

The very first inhabitants in Italy, over 150,000 years before the Romans, would have been cavemen relying solely on hunting for survival. In approximately 2000 BC, tribes from Central Europe and Asia began migrating to Italy and settled around Bologna. These people became known as the Villanovans. They settled in huts in small village communities and cultivated land and animals for their livelihood. The early farmers grew wheat and barley, made tools from iron, ate meat (goats and pigs) and, as they grew in numbers, moved south to Tuscany and Latium. The Villanovans culture grew and, by the eighth century BC, the Etruscans (still considered by some historians to be intruders from the East) sowed the seeds for a great civilization. The Etruscans, as their name suggests, were based in the province known today as Tuscany. This advanced civilization lived in urban settlements or small cities situated on high ground, well fortified against invasion (eg. Volterra p. 131 and Chiusi). Archaelogical remains have shown us a great deal of their way of life; the walls of some of the numerous tombs that have survived are covered with murals depicting men and women playing music, dancing and enjoying elaborate parties. Others show battle and hunting scenes. The Etruscans were brilliant workers in gold and other metals, ingenious inventors, sculptors in local alabaster. These crafts they traded with the Greeks who had by 750 BC colonized southern Italy and Sicily. The Greeks were the first people to cultivate the wild olives and vines that grew in abundance in Italy. They brought luxury goods to trade with from Greece, and their taste in architecture, but they did not stay long for civil wars at home kept them too busy to consider conquest.

11

The Etruscans moved south to develop the small latin village of Rome. They drained the swamp that was later to become the Forum Romana and constructed palaces and roads. The prosperity they created attracted many tribesmen from the neighbouring countryside. When the Etruscans went to war against the Greeks in the south, the Romans rebelled against their Etruscan masters and finally took Rome in 509 BC.

Over the next 200 years the republic of Rome conquered nearly all the Italian peninsula. Having unified Italy the Romans then spread their Empire over much of the known world.

The Late Empire was torn by barbarian invasions and civil wars and this led to the Roman Empire finally collapsing in the fifth century AD. It would be more than 1300 years before Italy came under unified rule once more.

The years between the late fifth and eighth centuries are usually termed the European Migration Period, as tribes clashed and feuded for territories. The Emperors of Constantinople, still in theory the governors of Italy, no longer had real control. They tried to regain it with the capture of Ravenna from the Goths in AD 540, but were thwarted by the strong Lombard warriors (German tribesmen from the Danube) who, in AD 568, invaded and conquered the regions that we know as Lombardy, Veneto and Tuscany.

The Lombards replaced the central government of Italy with local administrations called Duchys. Each Duchy was ruled by a Duke (Duce) who assumed the role similar to that of a King, his kingdom being divided amongst groups of related Lombard families. The Byzantines continued to control some provinces, as did the Pope in Rome, so the Lombard invasion hardened the divisions in the peninsula.

It was only a short time until the Pope was to clash (over a religious matter) with the Emperor in Constantinople, and so he organized a revolt against him. The Lombards joined in this revolt against the Emperor, not only to aid the Pope but to chase the Byzantines out of Italy. The Lombards had now conquered the Imperial Capital, Ravenna , and the Pope, Gregory the Great, faced with the possibility of an invasion of all the imperial territories by the Lombards, appealed to Pepin the Short, the French King, for help. Pepin invaded, reconquered the Imperial lands and gave them back to the Pope. In AD 774, (Charles the Great) Charlemagne, the son of Pepin, captured the

Lombard King and, in recognition, he was crowned the Holy Roman Emperor at St Peter's on Christmas Day AD 800.

For the next two to three hundred years, skirmishes continued. In AD 827, the Saracens invaded Sicily. In the early eleventh century, the Normans arrived in the south. However, in contrast to the south, central and northern Italy were slowly growing richer.

During the Middle Ages, although Italy's politics were confused, trade increased, especially from outside Europe, and so the maritime republics of Pisa, Genoa and Venice were born. The prosperity of inland cities also grew. Milan and Verona, because they lay at the gateway to the Alps; Bologna, because of its central position; and Florence, because of its access to Pisa and the sea via the river Arno.

However, under the rule of the Emperor Frederick II (1197–1250), a new quarrel arose between church and Empire and Italy became a civil battlefield once more. The 'Guelfs', supporters of Pope Gregory IX, and the 'Ghibellines', allies to Frederick, fought for supremacy. It was the Guelfs who eventually won to form an alliance between church and city states but by no means an unification. At the beginning of the fourteenth century, constant fighting in northern Italy ended when both the Emperor and Pope washed their hands of Italian affairs, and the region was freed from outside interference.

The Italian cities, already stronger and richer than any others in Europe, gained more and more power. Even the Black Death, which reduced the population by nearly fifty percent, did not stop the rising prosperity. The merchants brought artistry to commerce as they introduced double-entry book-keeping, holding companies and insurance institutions, the basis of modern business practice. With this wealth came a desire for art to glorify their cities; and so artists found patrons more easily, a crucial factor in the flourishing of the Renaissance in Italy. In small city states like that of San Gimignano in Tuscany, the prosperity soon led to jealousy and strife between noble families and in such places, to maintain rule, a one man leadership developed, i.e. dictatorship.

The cities of Venice, Florence, Lucca and Pisa never resorted to despotism, since their merchants were all very powerful and a balance was maintained. Florence was to become the most important city in Europe in the late fourteenth century. Its wealth and power were based in the wool trade, in particular a heavy red cloth which was in great demand all over Europe. A Wool Guild was formed called the 'Arte Della Lana' which, interestingly, paid out of its enormous profits for the construction and decoration of the cathedral in Florence.

Gradually the wealth and thus the power of the city states declined so that in the centuries that followed, the rule of Italy by Italians became almost a thing of the past, for the great states of Europe — France, Spain and Austria — divided up the peninsula between themselves. For a time Napoleon managed to bring it under his domination but even he was defeated in 1814. By 1830, Italy was divided into seven states: Lombardy, Venetia, Tuscany, Modena and Parma were controlled by Austria; the two Sicilies by the Bourbons (Spain); the Kingdom of Sardinia (including Piedmont), remained independent; and of course, the Papal States were ruled by the Pope.

With the independent Piedmontese, notably the revolutionary patriots Mazzini and Garibaldi, in the forefront Italy suffered four decades of battles and rebellions before the last of the foreign rulers was ejected and even the Papal States had decided to join the nation.

However, this unification did not mark the end of Italy's troublesome history. The southerners were wary of the newly founded northern government, and the Pope, although allowed to continue ruling the Vatican State, refused to acknowledge true unity until 1929.

In the Great War of 1914–1918, Italy was allied to England and France. In this century Italy's involvement in both World Wars has been particularly costly. In the fifties economically the south of Italy was desperate, and the originally thriving north was by no means as rich as the rest of Western Europe. This has now been overcome due to an industrial revolution in the last thirty years.

Today, Italy's greatest revenue comes from the export of all types of engineering products, backed up by increasing tourism, and its prosperity continues to grow.

Introduction to Tuscany

Marble Mountains

Agriculture and Produce

Tuscany is a region with a varied landscape and, therefore, difficult to describe in general terms, apart from the fact that it is very beautiful. It is characterized by cyprus trees and umbrella pines, in the centre, and imposing mountains to the north and south.

Its long coastline consists of rocks and beaches towards the north and, to the south, it widens out to a wildlife haven called The Maremma.

Although Tuscany's hillsides are difficult and expensive to cultivate, and they are not, in their natural state, particularly fertile, every conceivable clear space is put to use. An immense quantity of wheat (for bread and pasta), maize (for cattle feed and oil), sunflowers (for food and oil), olives and vines are grown on them very successfully.

On the plains, however, it is a different story. Ancient alluvial and volcanic deposits have created here a very fertile soil, ideal for sophisticated agriculture and in recent years, numerous market gardens have appeared producing every type of fruit and vegetable imaginable.

In some parts, the Tuscan landscape still remains untamed, and rocky hills covered with beech and chestnut make a natural hunting ground. The woods are full of wild delicacies and game (venison and truffles for example), which will eventually find themselves on the dining room tables of houses and restaurants throughout the region.

Regional Fungi

Wild Mushrooms
Porcini — These wonderful edible fungi, best known to us as the Cep, are dark brown with large heads like old fashioned buns. For centuries continental housewives have regarded the Cep as being the most useful of edible fungi. In Tuscany these flourish in the natural woodland, and after the rain in late Summer and early Autumn, you will see the locals out collecting them in wicker baskets.

17

Porcini, or Morecci as they are sometimes called, can be used in many forms of cooking and dry well. Fresh they are quite delightful, just sliced, coated with flour and lightly fried in olive oil.

Ovoli — The Ovoli or Cocchi is an orange skinned mushroom. It is used mainly raw in salads, dressed with olive oil, lemon and salt.

Menine — A beige to yellow mushroom used in sauces.

Truffles — Tartufi

These underground Fungi belong to the division of the Ascomycetes. They have much the same appearance as potatoes, but their structure is entirely different. When old they become full of brown spores, much like puffballs, but when young they are fleshy in texture. Several species are edible. The best ones are to be found in natural oak woodland in Tuscany. They are grey and are called *Il grigio d'Alba*.

These extraordinary underground mushrooms grow round certain types of oak trees. Having no stem or root they can only be detected by the faint smell they give off. To unearth these treasures, the digger needs a mate with a keener sense of smell than himself. In ancient times pigs were used, but today special dogs sniff out these very expensive delicacies.

Olives and Olive Oil — Olive e Olio d'Oliva

Italy is the world's leading producer of olives and olive oil. Olives come in numerous varieties, sizes and colours; yellow, black, green and purple, and are not just reserved to be nibbled with aperitifs, but are used a great deal in cooking.

The best olive oil comes from Lucca in Tuscany. This oil is heavier, fruitier and stronger, both in colour and flavour, than the oils from the rest of Italy. It is made from hand-picked green olives, and is virtually the basis for every Tuscan dish. If you are under the impression that it will be cheap in Italy, then I am afraid that you will be very disappointed. Make sure you buy the very best *extra vergine* oil to bring back home, it is most definitely worth the extra lire.

Rice — Riso

Rice in Tuscany, no surely not, it is only grown in the Po! Well, much to our surprise, as we were driving along the superstrada just south of Siena, we were confronted by fields of rice stretching out on either side of the road.

This grain, which requires a lot of water and heat for ripening, would not have found a favourable habitat here if it were not for the ingenuity of a brilliant man, whose name I have been unable to discover. With government sponsorship, he graded the ground and designed a brilliant irrigation system to suit the production of this highly sought after crop. The system allows the ground to be flooded or drained at will by means of sluices and pumping stations.

After ploughing in winter, the paddy fields are planted out in the spring (nowadays mechanically). The crop grows throughout the summer months when the plant is a beautiful shade of green. By late September the fields are drained and the grain is allowed to ripen and dry. When the husks are golden in colour, the harvesting begins.

Main Local Produce

PRODUCE	SEASON/where applicable
Fruit	
PEACHES *Pesche*	August
APRICOTS *Albicocche*	June/mid-July
FIGS *Fichi*	late September
2 types green & black (nero)	
APPLES *Mela*	Autumn
GRAPES *Uva*	late September
— Edible	10th October onwards
— Wine	depending on weather
PEARS *Pere*	late September
CHERRIES *Ciliege*	early to mid-June

cont.

PRODUCE	SEASON/where applicable
STRAWBERRIES *Fragole*	June
MELONS *Melone*	Summer
BLACKBERRIES *More*	Autumn
TOMATOES *Pomodori**	

— San Marzano — Plum shaped which ripen early, ideal for cooking

— Sangiovannino — small cherry tomatoes. (These are hung in bunches to dry in a cool place and will last through the winter.)

Nuts

WALNUTS *Noci*	Mid-September, will keep until Christmas
HAZELNUTS *Noccioline*	Autumn
ALMONDS *Mandorle*	Mid-October
CHESTNUTS *Marrone* or *Castagne*	late Autumn/Winter

Olive

OLIVE *Olive*	November/December

Edible Fungi

MUSHROOMS

— *Porcini* or *Morecci*	late Summer/early Autumn
— *Ovoli* or *Cocchi*	best to collect after
— *Menine* (yellow)	the rain
TRUFFLES *Tartuffi*	end September to March

Herbs

FENNEL SEEDS *Sem di finocchio*
WILD ROSEMARY *Rosemarino*
GARLIC *Aglio*
CLOVES *Chiodi di Garofano*
JUNIPER *Gineprio*

Cereals

WHEAT *Grano*	harvesting starts early in May
RICE *Riso*	October

* Named by a sixteenth-century Sienese physician, 'Pomo d'oro' (golden apples), because the first tomatoes to arrive in Italy from the Aztecs were yellow.

PRODUCE	SEASON/where applicable

Vegetables
WHITE BEANS *Fagioli*   Summer
ARTICHOKES *Carciofi*   Winter/early Spring
AUBERGINE *Melanzane*   September
FENNEL *Finocchio*

Meat
WHITE BEEF CATTLE *Bistecca*   all year round, from Chiana Valley, Italy's
  alla Fiorentina   best T-bone steaks
PORK *Maiali*   best in Winter

Poultry
CHICKEN *Pollo*   all year round, Italy's best are from Leghorn —
                        Livorno — and have yellow legs
QUAILS *Qauglia*   all year round

Fish
SALT COD *Baccala*
TROUT *Trotta*   from mountain rivers and lakes
RED MULLET *Triglie*   from Leghorn

Game
The season starts on the 20th September and goes through until the 20th March. Game hunting is only permitted on three days of the week: Sunday, Wednesday and Thursday. The other days are reserved for collecting truffles, mushrooms and other wild produce, without the risk of being shot. Each year, Tuscans are killed during the game season.

BABY DEER *Cappriolo*
VENISON *Cervo*
PHEASANT *Fagiano*
HARE *Lepre*
WILD PIGEON *Colombo*
WILD BOAR *Cinghiale*
THRUSH *Tordo*
BLACKBIRD *Merlo*

Crafts

Marble

Definition: 'Marble is a metaphoric rock (limestone) which has become entirely crystalline by the operation of heat, pressure or sometimes both'.

It is the presence of certain minerals in marble which give it its beautiful and varied subtle colours. It is only if the limestone was originally pure that marble is white. The best marbles come from Italy, the finest of all around Massa and Carrara in the Apuane Alps.

In Michelangelo's day, chisels and wooden wedges were used to procure chunks of this wonderful substance. Today, explosives help to open the natural cracks between the faces. Water and sand, which has an abrasive action, are then flushed through the grooves of steel cables used for quarrying and the blocks are then transported down to the plain where they are cut or dressed in factories and workshops by highly skilled craftsmen.

Alabaster

There are two different minerals to which the name Alabaster has been given.

1) In Etruscan and ancient times, Alabaster, named after the town called Alabastron in Egypt, was a hard marble-like Calcite or crystalline calcium carbonate of lime, and was much in demand for ornamental purposes. Little of this type is left today.

2) The alabaster most common now is a naturally occurring form of gypsum, a hydrated sulphate of lime. This is a much softer mineral and slightly soluble in water. It has a number of commercial purposes and can be used for ornamental work and sculpture. Burnt gypsum is known as plaster of Paris, since it was first obtained from the Montmartre district in France.

Great quantities of alabaster have always been present in Tuscany, the

Appenines being limestone, but in particular around Volterra. Millions of years ago the valleys here were seas and inland lakes and, as the water evaporated, they left behind deposits of gypsum.

Alabaster is quarried conventionally in this region, by power driven cutters and extracted in large rectangular or egg-shaped blocks, some of which weigh several tons. The blocks are sold either to mills, run by co-operatives, or to individual craftsmen. It is shaped or turned on lathes into plates, columns and numerous other very saleable items. These pieces will normally be white and translucent but can be individually dyed or polished to achieve different finishes.

Early Art and Architecture

Tuscans have devoted to all the various branches of art more labour and study than all the other Italian peoples.

Vasari

The earliest art to be found in Tuscany is that of the Etruscans. They were heavily influenced by the Orient and Greece, and the art we see is tied closely to images of death. Etruscans believed strongly in the afterlife. Colourful frescoes showing athletic contests, grand parties and conquests can be seen in their tombs, together with splendid funeral objects made of gold and beautifully sculpted alabaster cinerary urns.

To the Etruscans, death was the ultimate honour and to remind the dead solely of good times, they would decorate and furnish their tombs. Examples of tomb art and the bronze statuette *Al'ombra della sera* (In the evening shadow) are exhibited in the Musea Etrusco in Volterra.

In the field of architecture, we know little except that they invented the 'true arch', that is an arch made from wedge-shaped stones and the 'barrel vault' a continuous arched vault of semicircular section.

Of the more celebrated Roman architecture, unfortunately, little remains in the cities of Tuscany, except for some ruins of Roman baths and amphitheatres such as those discovered in Volterra in 1950. Reminders, however, are left in Lucca, where an elliptical Piazza has been built on the site of the amphitheatre, and in Florence, near the Santa Croce, where the streets wind in a manner that almost follows the perimeter of the ancient theatre. Other Roman remains can be found along the Tuscan coastline, proving that its natural beauty made it a favoured place to stay even in Roman times.

To many a visit to Tuscany is a pilgrimage to the cradle of Renaissance culture. The achievements of that era are too numerous to summarize adequately here, instead we offer you a selection of some of the great names of Tuscany.

Important Tuscans

Fra Angelico (c. 1400–1455)
Fra Angelico is the name by which the painter, Guido di Petro, is best known. He was born in Tuscany and became a Dominican friar at the age of 20. He took the name Fra Giovanni da Fiesola but was known as the Blessed Angelico because of his saintly character and the beauty of his nature.

He was the first Italian artist to paint a landscape that can be identified (Lake Trasimeno seen from Cortona).

Giovanni Boccaccio (1313–1375)
This Italian poet was the son of a Florentine merchant. His great work was the *Decameron*. He was a friend of Petrarch and sponsored Leon Pilatus' translation of Homer.

Sandro Botticelli (1444–1510)
Botticelli was not his real name for he was christened Alessandro di Mariano dei Filipepi, but his brother's nickname 'Botticelli' meaning 'Little Barrel' was passed on to him.

His father was a tanner and Sandro was first apprenticed to a goldsmith, and then, turning to painting, he became apprenticed to Fra Filippo Lippi and subsequently was patronized by the Medici family. *The Birth of Venus* hangs in the Uffizi, Florence.

Fillipo Brunelleschi (1377–1446)
A pioneer of the early Renaissance whose mathematical definition of perspective became a major artistic tool. His architectural credits include the immense dome of Florence Cathedral and the Pitti Palace.

Giosue Carducci (1835–1907)
This Tuscan poet was appointed Professor of Italian Literature in Bologna in 1860. His *Inno a Satana* (Hymn to Satan, 1865) is full of revolutionary feeling. He was awarded the Nobel Prize for Literature in 1906.

Carlo Collodi (1826–1890)
Carol Collodi is the pseudonym of the Italian writer Carlo Lorenzini, adopted from the birthplace of his mother.

He was born in Florence where he became a journalist. He is best remembered for his book *The Adventure of Pinocchio* which he wrote between 1881-3.

Alighieri Dante (1265–1321)
Hailed as one of the greatest poets of the Middle Ages, the author of *The Divine Comedy* was born in Florence into a highly respected family. He became a scholar of repute and took an active part in the politics of his native city. When his enemies came to power, he was banished and died in Ravenna in Eastern Italy.

Donatello (Donato di Niccolo di Betto Bardi) (1386–1466)
Donatello was a native of Florence. Of him Vasari said, 'Donatello aimed so high and achieved so much that he may be said to have been one of the first in modern times to shed light, by his practice, judgement and knowledge, on the art of sculpture and good design.'

The classical bronze statue *David* is at Florence (one of the earliest of Renaissance independent nudes) and *St John* is at Siena Cathedral.

25

Duccio (di Buonninsegna) (c. 1255-1319)

Duccio was the first great Sienese painter and he stands in relation to the Sienese School as Giotto does to the Florentine.

His greatest work is his altarpiece for Siena Cathedral (1308-11). Two of his pupils Simone Martini (c. 1284-1344) and Lippo Memmi together painted *The Annunciation* for an altar in Siena Cathedral. It is now in the Uffizi Gallery, Florence. Martini also painted a portrait of Laura, beloved of Petrarch.

Galileo Galilei (1564–1642)

This great Italian scientist and astronomer is nearly always known by his first name, Galileo. He was born at Pisa, the son of a musician, and was sent to school at the monastery of Vallombrosa, near Florence. In 1581 he entered the University of Pisa where he studied first medicine and later mathematics and science. Legend has it that whilst watching a lantern swinging to and fro Galileo realized that each swing took almost exactly the same time and so conceived the use of a pendulum to measure time.

He became a lecturer in mathematics at Pisa University in 1589 where, whilst watching an opponent's demonstration of dropping two stones of unequal weight from the top of the Leaning Tower, he confirmed his view that all falling bodies, great or small, descend with equal velocity. This made him very unpopular with orthodox scientists and he left Pisa in 1591.

He became Professor of mathematics at Padua in 1592 where he remained until 1610.

In 1609, Galileo learned of the invention of the telescope by Hans Lippershey in Holland. He immediately built his own telescope and was the first to apply it to astronomy. It was then that he made a series of spectacular discoveries. He found the satellites of Jupiter, saw the craters of the Moon, the phases of Venus and the faint stars of the Milky Way.

His telescope was a refractor, i.e. it collected its light by means of a glass lens, and was feeble in comparison to modern standards with a magnification of only 32.

His observations led him to accept the Copernican System that the Sun, not the Earth, is the centre of the solar system and that the planets all revolve round it, which he advocated in his *Dialogues on the Two Principal Systems of the*

Universe. The book was banned on its publication in 1632 and Galileo was summoned to Rome by the Inquisition and ordered, under threat of torture, to recant his views. This he eventually did and was permitted to return to his home on condition that he did not leave it.

He went blind in 1637, but continued to work up to his death in 1642.

Giotto (di Bondone) (1266/7–1337)
Born at Vespignano, north of Florence, little is known of Giotto's early life but he was probably either a shepherd or an apprentice in the wool trade. Later he became a pupil of Cimabue. Giotto is chiefly famous for his frescoes in churches at Assisi, Padua and Florence and for his collaboration with Andrea Pisano in decorating the facade of the Cathedral in Florence with statues. The *Defeat of the Sultan's Priests* is in the Bardi Chapel of Santa Croce, Florence. He was also responsible for the conception and first zone of Florence's magnificent Campanile, which is named after him.

Fra Filippo Lippi (c. 1406–69)
Born in Florence, Fra Filippo Lippi was probably the only direct pupil of Masaccio. He was an orphan and was put into the Carmine in Florence in 1421, but he was temperamentally unsuited to being a monk.

His most important works are the frescoes in the choir of the Cathedral at Prato which were begun in 1452 and were still incomplete in 1464. Meanwhile Lippi was tried for fraud (1450) and he abducted a nun, Lucrezia, which resulted in the birth of his son, Filippino. The Medici family, his patrons, secured a dispensation for him to marry Lucrezia.

His last works were the frescoes in Spoleto Cathedral.

Niccolo Machiavelli (1469–1537)
Little is known of Machiavelli's early life, but both parents belonged to the city state of Florence, where his father was a well known lawyer.

Machiavelli was born in Florence. He was Second Chancellor to the Republic from 1498 until 1512. With the accession to power of the Medici in 1512, he was arrested. After being imprisoned and tortured, he was allowed to retire to his villa. He then spent his time writing; his most famous works were *The Prince* (1513), *L'Arte della Guerra* (1520), *Historie Fiorentine*, and *Discorsi* (1531).

Lorenzo de Medici (1449–92)
Known as 'The Magnificent', Lorenzo was a munificent patron of the arts and literature. Although not as skilled in politics and business as his grandfather, Cosimo, he, however, practically managed to become a dictator by using violence and cunning.

He was also a poet of considerable ability and persuaded writers of his time to use their native language, Italian, instead of Latin. He was patron to Michelangelo and under his rule Florence became the cultural centre of Europe.

Michelangelo (Buonarroti) (1475–1564)
Originally from a poor but genteel Tuscan family, Michelangelo was apprenticed to the Florentine Domenico Ghirlandajo (1449–1494). As with Leonardo he was absorbed by the problems of representing the human body and spent many hours dissecting. Although the Sistine Chapel is beyond the boundaries of Tuscany his 'David' is to be seen in the Accademia, Florence.

It was by permission of the Pope (his one-time patron) that Michelangelo travelled to the marble quarries at Carrara (see p. 74). Here he spent six months selecting the blocks from which he would create, amongst other works, the 'David'.

Benito Mussolini (1883–1945)
The son of a blacksmith, Mussolini was born in the Romagna. He was expelled from school for stabbing a fellow pupil, and in early adulthood he worked as a teacher and journalist, while becoming active in the Socialist movement, from which he was also expelled.

In 1919, he founded the 'Fasci di Combattimento', an extremist group, which launched a campaign of terrorism against the Socialists. Through this organisation, backed by many landowners and industrialists, police and army leaders, Mussolini eventually assumed dictatorial powers in 1925.

He embarked on a career of conquest: invaded Ethiopia in 1935-6, intervened in the Spanish Civil War of 1936-9 and conquered Albania in 1939.

Following his alliance with Nazi Germany, Mussolini had to contend with extreme discontent among his own people and was finally forced to resign in

July 1943 and was imprisoned. He was released from his internment by German parachutists in September 1943 and set up a 'Republican Fascist' government in Northern Italy. However, in 1945, he and his mistress were captured by partisans while trying to flee the country and were shot.

Francesco Petrarch (1304–1374)
This Italian poet and scholar was born at Arezzo. In 1313 he was taken to Avignon where he studied law and in 1326 he was ordained and entered the service of the Colonnas.

He was crowned poet in Rome in 1341 and was inspired by the greatness of Ancient Rome. He wrote *Il Canzoniere* sonnets in praise of Laura, *Africa* a Latin epic on Scipio the Elder and many philosophical treatises. He died at Arqua, near Padua.

Andrea Pisano (1270–1348)
Andrea Pisano was the assumed name of the Italian sculptor, Andrea da Pontaderra. His most famous work is one of the bronze doors of the Baptistry in Florence which he began in 1330 and finished in 1336. The only other works associated with him are, possibly, some statues on the Campanile of Florence Cathedral.

Giacomo Puccini (1858–1924)
The Puccini family lived in the Tuscan village of Celle, above Lucca, from at least the beginning of the sixteenth century. Celle, unlike Lucca which lies on a broad plain, is perched high on a sharp peak over the Roggio valley, at the top of a steep and dizzying narrow road. Thanks to a newly founded Luccan organization and the generosity of Puccini's niece, Alba Del Panta, the Puccini house has been carefully restored and is now a fascinating museum. A trip here is a must for opera lovers.

Sometime in the early eighteenth century, a member of this musical family moved down to the city of Lucca, where the first Giacomo was born in 1712. It is, however, the later musician of the same name, born in Lucca in 1858, who reached world renown with such operas as *La Boheme* (1896), *Tosca* (1900) and *Madame Butterfly* (1904). Despite his international success he returned frequently to Tuscany. Not to Lucca where his relationship with Elvira Bonturi, a married woman, caused problems with the conservative Lucchesi but to a villa he had built on the shores of Lake Massaciuccoli at Torre del Lago. The villa contains his piano, on which he composed *Madame Butterfly*, signed photographs of artists and friends and many other interesting souvenirs. Outside, regrettably, there are no longer peaceful views of a quiet lake bordered by reeds and full of wild fowl, instead you will see all the signs of modern tourism and civilization. Puccini, himself, was forced out of this hermitage in the early 1900s, for even in his time, Torre fell victim to modern peat extraction and subsequently to the factory.

From here he moved to Viareggio (a place now spoilt in favour of tourism) where he wrote *Turandot*. Viareggio was to be his last place of rest, for in November, 1924, he left there for Brussels hoping that, at the clinic of the brilliant Dr Ledoox, his life could be saved by an operation for throat cancer. The operation was unsuccessful and he died on November 4th, 1924.

'Verdi, ah yes, Verdi is great, universal: his operas will go on forever. But when I die, what will be left of me?' Giacomo Puccini.

Catherine of Siena (1347–80)

This Catholic Saint and mystic was born at Siena. Fervently religious from childhood, at the age of 16 she became a Dominican tertiary. She attempted to reconcile the Florentines with the Pope and persuaded Gregory XI to return to Rome from Avignon in 1376.

In 1375, she is said to have received on her body, the Stigmata, the impression of Christ's five wounds. Her *Dialogue* is a remarkable mystical work. She was canonized in 1461.

Giorgio Vasari (1511–74)

Vasari was born in Arezzo and trained in Florence.

He was a superb impressario rather than a painter, and his work as an architect ranks much higher. But his fame mainly rests on his book *Le Vite de piu Eccellenti Architetti, Pittori et Scultori Italiani* first published in 1550 and updated to a much larger version in 1568.

Leonardo da Vinci (1452-1519)

Leonardo was born at Vinci, the illegitimate son of a Florentine notary. He was brought up in his father's house and trained as a painter, traditionally under Verrochio (1435-1488). Da Vinci is frequently described as the finest example of a Renaissance man because of the variety of his talents. He studied the workings of the human body more deeply than most doctors of his day and theorised on the circulation of the blood. He is credited with the invention of the first armoured fighting vehicle, projected several aircraft and helicopters and anticipated the submarine.

He began work as an independent artist in about 1477 under the patronage of Lorenzo the Magnificent. In 1482, he was employed by Lodovico Sforza at Milan as state engineer, court painter and director of court festivities. He later became chief engineer to Duke Cesare Borgia.

The Mona Lisa, *La Giocondo*, is probably the most famous painting in the world. He died in France at Cloux, near Amboise, in a château given to him by King Louis XII.

CAFÉ

The Epicure's Guide

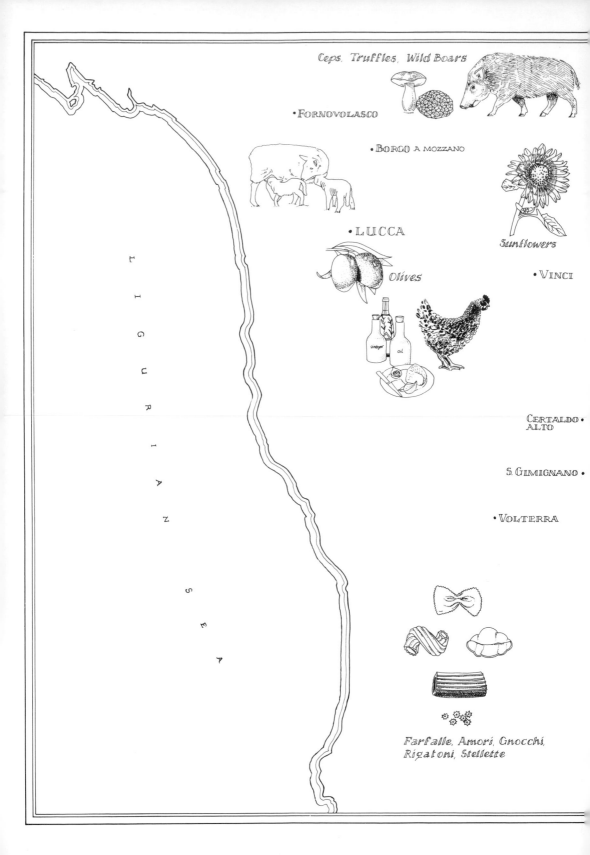

Ceps, Truffles, Wild Boars

• FORNOVOLASCO

• BORGO A MOZZANO

Sunflowers

• LUCCA

Olives

• VINCI

CERTALDO •
ALTO

S. GIMIGNANO •

• VOLTERRA

LIGURIAN SEA

Farfalle, Amori, Gnocchi,
Rigatoni, Stellette

EPICURE'S GUIDE
TUSCANY

Ceps, Truffles, Wild Boars

• FLORENCE
(FIRENZE)

Maize
Wheat
Chianina

• PANZANO

• AREZZO

• SIENA

Panforte
Rice

• CASTIGLIONE

• MONTEPULCIANO

• MONTALCINO

Ceps, Truffles, Wild Boars

Rice

Food

Historically, the Italians are believed to have taught the art of cuisine to the French, however, in all my travels the only evidence of this that I could find was in the number of courses that one is expected to go through on the menu, and the many varieties of charcuterie, meats, and cheese available.

There is much more to Italian food than the legendary pasta, pizza and ice cream. So if you are a devout carnivore, like my husband Innes, never fear. Florentine beef steak is the best in Italy and is ordered by the 100 gram so you can gorge yourself on the largest piece the chef can find. I suppose I ought to mention that you pay per 100 grams too, but who cares, you're on holiday.

If you happen to be a pasta fiend like myself, there are endless types to try. The Italians boast over 200 different pasta shapes, and some of the elaborate sauces that accompany them are quite delicious. A typically Tuscan dish is Pappardelle alla Lepre, strips of home-made pasta with hare sauce. The only disappointment is that pasta is traditionally served as a second course and therefore the portions are understandably smaller than one might expect.

Pizzas are, of course, excellent. They emerge from proper brick ovens, crispy and sizzling, and as for ice creams, Italy's must rate as the best in the world. We found a Gelateria (ice-cream shop) in Florence that had no less than 84 varieties!

Eating out for Italians is a family occasion and is more like a ceremony than just a meal, especially on high days and holidays. When choosing a restaurant, where the food is usually more interesting than in your hotel, follow the usual tourist rule and pick one which is full of locals, the food will be good and the atmosphere lively. However, Italians do tend to eat dinner late and so my advice is to savour your 'aperitivo' and delay eating until 8.30 or 9.00 p.m.

At first sight the menu may be bewildering, however good your Italian, since the names of dishes can vary from region to region, and local dishes can have very strange names.

The first course is the antipasti or appetizer. These vary in quantity and content from a simple plate of salamis and mountain hams, hand cut off the bone, to a huge selection of interesting and tasty dishes. These may include wafer-thin meats served with melon or figs; mixed fish salad; local game sausages; Mortadella; salamis; liver and/or mushroom patés on fried bread; and pickled vegetables, garnished with olives and fresh tomatoes. An antipasti like this certainly rates highly in my estimation, but is not the norm everywhere.

Next on the menu comes the heading: Zuppe e Pasta. Pasta and Risotto (which is also included here) are basically self explanatory, with the exception of regional recipes which will be explained later; but Zuppe can be slightly misleading in Tuscany. Generally speaking, Zuppe means soup and you will find minestra, consomme and cream soups on many menus, but Zuppe is also the word used for a Tuscan speciality of peasant origin, which is a wholesome dish containing vegetables, pulses and bread. Quite delectable but thoroughly filling.

Then comes the main course or 'Secondi' Piatti which consists of a choice of meat or fish. If you are feeling thoroughly daunted by the thought of all these courses, take heart — it is considered polite to miss out one starter, but to miss out both could be taken as an insult. The Italians don't often go in for mouthwatering sauces like their French neighbours, so many dishes will be simply roasted or grilled.

Vegetables and salads must be ordered separately and are, in my opinion, sadly lacking in imagination when you consider how many unusual vegetables and salad items are produced and are, indeed, available in the markets and shops in Tuscany. Do not expect them to be piping hot. On the contrary they are often tepid or cold and arrive after the meat. If you wish everything to be served together, my advice is to ask the waiter when you order. In September and October, Porcini, wild mushrooms, appear on many Tuscan menus and are thoroughly recommended.

I have already mentioned that Italy makes an enormous range of cheese. In restaurants, though, the cheese board is not generally elaborate. A small selection of local sheep or goats' milk cheeses will be offered.

Desserts do not take up much room on menus either. Ice creams, if they are home-made, are always good especially topped with liqueur cherries.

Panforte, a rich cake from Siena (see p. 43) is interesting to try; and fresh fruit is always at hand.

Finally we come to coffee. The Italians drink either very strong small espresso, or Capuccino, whisked with hot foamy milk and topped in the traditional manner with grated chocolate.

Shops and Specialities

The Baker — Panettiere, Panificio, Fornaio

In the Baker's shop you will find excellent fresh bread of all different shapes and types, for the Italians consume more bread than any other nation.

In Italy, bakers bake at least six days a week, if not seven, and a great deal of bread, especially in Tuscany, is still baked in wood-fired ovens, similar to those used for pizza. Loaves vary in size from enormous to the thin sticks known as Grissini, which taste far better fresh than the ones we get over here in plastic wrappers.

Tuscan bread is made without salt. Legend has it that during the Middle Ages, salt was highly taxed by the Pope so, to keep the price down, it was simply cut out of the recipe and the tradition has continued to this day.

The Butcher — Macelleria

Most butchers in small towns and villages slaughter their own meat, so the choice will depend on availability. Generally speaking though, the butcher will sell beef, veal, lamb, kid, pork and offal. Salamis and hams will be sold in alimentari or salumeria, and poultry and game in separate shops, at the market or in the supermarket (supermercato). It would be quite impossible to describe all the cuts of meat here, since they are so different from ours, but they are usually nice and lean. If you happen to be self-catering, you will find it easier to tell the butcher what dish you are preparing and he will sell you the appropriate cut.

Beef: Manzo, but in Tuscany it is sold as Vitellone
Tuscany produces the best breed of cattle in Italy. This special breed 'the Chianina' is reared solely for eating. They are pure alabaster in colour and grow up to weigh about 400 lbs. Their meat 'Vitellone' is certainly beautifully tender, but is neither true beef nor true veal.

Veal: Vitello, but in Tuscany it is sometimes called Vitella
Veal should be meat from a calf of two or three months old. However, more often than not, in Tuscany veal is darker in colour than one would expect because it comes from the Chianina cattle. Vitello al latte, which is milk fed and almost white in colour, is the name given to the meat that we know as veal and is used for Italy's famous veal escalopes.

Lamb: Agnello
Lamb rarely appears on a menu in Tuscany, except north of Lucca, where the climate is less arid. Young milk fed lambs, however, are reared ready to grace the Tuscan table on Christmas Day.

Kid: Capretto
Kid, on the other hand, is a great Italian favourite and is eaten with considerable enthusiasm. They are sold whole and should be no bigger than 5-6 kg.

Pork: Maiale
The Italians produce two breeds of pig. The first is allowed to grow to a monstrous size and is turned into tasty hams, sausages, salamis and bacon. The second is a much smaller breed and is used for roasting. Although pork is cheap in Italy, it is essentially a winter meat.

Offal: Frattaglie
Liver (fegato), brains (cervella) and tripe (trippa) have always been a favourite of the Italian housewife, and there are many recipes for them. The Italians also eat parts of the animal which we usually throw away; for example, calf's head and feet are considered to be delicacies and are used in special soups and stews.

The Delicatessen — Alimentari or Salumeria

These shops are fascinating and are crammed with an incredible selection of tempting foods. Hams and salamis hang from the ceiling; trays of freshly made pasta, salads and home-made local dishes are displayed in the chilled cabinet; shelves are stacked with preserved vegetables, purées, herbs, olives, vinegars and oils; and any remaining space is taken up with cheese, special cakes and wine. The ideal shop in which to buy the basis for a wonderful picnic.

Meat Products

There are literally dozens of salamis, sausages and hams, in Italy, all regional. The list below is not comprehensive but may give you some guidelines.

1. *Mortadella*
Again there are lots of varieties. The best Mortadella is thought to come from Bologna in Emilia-Romagna and not from Tuscany. This sausage is pink and dotted with cubes of hard white pork fat and/or pistachio nuts. Personally, I think it is one of Italy's nicest cold meats.

2. *Carpaccio*
Very thinly sliced raw topside or fillet of beef. Serve with fresh lemon juice, olive oil and black pepper. Even if you abhor raw meat, this is worth a try for the lemon and olive oil seem to semi-cook it.

3. *Bresaola*
Cured dried fillet of beef, served in thick slices.

4. *Coppiette*
A Tuscan speciality. Dried smoked wild boar, very expensive.

5. *Pancetta*
Unsmoked salted streaky bacon, cured with spices and rolled up like a salami. In recipes, it is either cubed, or thinly sliced. Can be eaten raw.

6. *Prosciutto (crudo-raw)*
This is the general name for all salted and air-cured raw hams. The most

famous is, of course, the one from Parma, but Tuscany's mountain hams — Prosciutto di Montagna — can be just as good.

Prosciutto (cotto-cooked)
Cooked ham is available but is not so popular since it lacks taste.

7. *Salame*
Strictly translated this is a raw salt-cured sausage which again comes in endless regional varieties. It can be made from pork, wild boar, venison and even duck. In Tuscany the salami are often flavoured with fennel seeds.

8. *Sausages*
These are far too numerous to list, and also come with various fillings and flavourings. In Tuscany game ones are popular, so these are the type I suggest you try; just ask in the deli.

Cheese — Formaggio

Italy claims to make more cheese than France. There are over 400 cheeses listed in France and many more unrecorded, so if this is true, Italy must make a very great number indeed. Every region and many villages have their own speciality; look out for ones labelled 'nostrano' meaning local or ours. These will generally be made with goat's or ewe's milk by the local peasant farmer. Tuscany's two best known cheeses are Pecorino, a strong salty cheese with a hard rind and Caciotta, smallish round cheeses made from a mixture of ewe's and cow's milk.

The Poultry Shop — Polleria

These shops specialise in poultry and will sell a huge variety of fresh birds from large turkeys right down to the smallest quail. They will also sell rabbits and game, in season. Tuscany has a reputation for the finest chickens in Italy and, therefore, some of its best-known traditional recipes are based on this bird. Quail is also popular and is cooked with succulent white grapes.

The Cake Shop — Pasticceria

The Cake Shop, as in every country, is a den of iniquity. If you are worried about the waistline then hurry past their extremely tempting window displays.

Cake shops don't just sell rich cakes either, but sweets and chocolates too, and biscuits which the Italians dip into their sweet dessert wines. All yummy, yummy!

Tuscany's most famous cake comes from Siena and is called 'Panforte'. It is a large flat cake made with grapes, figs, honey, spices, cloves, cinnamon and nuts. These days there are several varieties, but the classic black Panforte is made from the original recipe invented by monks in the Middle Ages.

The Ice Cream Parlour — Gelateria

This is the place to buy the best ice-cream and water ice in the world.

Italians have indulged themselves in this fabulous food since Roman times. It is recorded that Roman Emperors sent their slaves to collect snow from the Apennines to flavour and consume. Today, thanks to progress you can enjoy a much more refined product. Both water ice (granita) and ice-cream (gelato) can be sampled at their very best from Gelateria displaying the sign 'Produzione Propria' (home-made) outside. You will, of course, be spoilt for choice, since over 20% of Italy's entire fruit production goes into ice-cream, but whichever flavours you choose, I can assure you that they will be quite scrumptious.

Fiona Fennell

Wine

"In the Italian feast wine plays the chief supporting role".

Hugh Johnson

Wine is a way of life in Italy, and Tuscany is the land of the vine. Both in the home and in restaurants, it will be present on the table at every meal, and even the smallest bambini will partake, all be it in a very watery form.

Italy has been making wine for centuries, even before the Romans, and is now the largest producer in the world. Apart from extensive organised viticulture, practically every Tuscan family and many restaurateurs will grow enough vines to service their yearly needs. If you are adventurous, these local wines are definitely the most interesting to sample, but beware, as one might expect, they vary tremendously in style and taste. At the very worst, they can be rough, nasty and acid, but at their best, they are smooth and palatable. Anyway, luckily, these 'Vino Locale' are incredibly cheap, so whatever your reaction, they are worth a try and add to the fun of your holiday.

Within Italy, wines don't travel much anyway and so you will find the locally grown wine heads the menu. When in Montepulciano, Chianti, San Gimignano or Montalcino, follow the local's choice. Drink the wine of the region and you won't go far wrong. Incidentally it will also go best with the food.

Please don't stop at too many 'enoteche' for serious tastings, since Italian roads seem to be all bends and I want you to enjoy your travels to the full.

The only other point I would like to mention before I give you a brief outline of the wine districts you will visit in Tuscany, is to remember to try Italy's 'Holy Wine' or 'Vin Santo' as the finale to your meal.

Remember the only way to increase your knowledge of wine is to drink it — Salute!

Chianti

Chianti is perhaps the best known wine in Tuscany and one of the most popular, coming from the hills between Florence and Siena. Chianti is the largest D.O.C. area in the whole of Italy and is divided into seven zones as follows: Classico, Colli Aretini, Colli Fiorentino, Colli Senesi, Colline Pisane, Montalbano and Rufina. It is, therefore, a huge family of red and white wines of varying qualities. The red variety is the best and by far the most popular, being made from a blend of red Sangiovese and Canailo grapes, and white Trebbiano and Malvasia grapes, a formula that was devised early in the nineteenth century.

The best are labelled 'classico' or 'Riserva' and, if they have been left to age for some five to six years in oak casks, are full bodied and resemble a French claret. These wines will always have the seal of the black cockerel on the neck, should be served at room temperature, allowed to breathe and are a good accompaniment to red meat and game.

Vernaccia di San Gimignano

Vernaccia comes from the latin 'Vernaculus' meaning 'native' or 'of this place', so it is a term given to wines all over Italy. However, it is the dry wine from San Gimignano, one of my favourite Tuscan white wines, that we will discuss here.

These vineyards cover about 400 hectares (1000 acres) of hillside around this picturesque town and produce some 26,000 hectolitres of wine. This wine, which is hardly known in England today, was, interestingly, drunk in medieval London when it was called Vernage.

The grapes, which are high in acidity, produce an easily recognisable interesting wine of great character. Golden in colour and lightly chilled, it goes perfectly with anti-pasta and shell-fish.

Vino Nobile di Montepulciano

Certainly one of Italy's best red wines and full of body. Vino Nobile must have been aged for at least two years to conform to the D.O.C.G. ruling, but if aged for three years, it may be awarded the title of riserva, and after four years riserva speciale. It is an unusual, if not heavy, wine to be drunk with roast meat or cheese.

Brunello di Montalcino (D.O.C.G.)

'Brunello' — little dark one. A lesser known wine but nonetheless rich and powerful in flavour, good with game, and solely made in the small village of Montalcino near Siena.

The Italians class it as one of their most prestigious wines and consider ten years to be a good age. Especially good are those made by Biondi-Santi whose family first produced Brunello over one hundred years ago.

Try also Rosso di Montalcino (D.O.C.), a lighter fresher wine from the same Sangiovese Grosso grape.

It is important to serve both these wines at room temperature, and if they are old, allow them to breathe for at least twenty minutes.

Vin Santo or 'Holy Wine'

A strong dessert wine made from semi-dried grapes, a long slow fermentation and many years of ageing.

It is normally sweet, but when dry it has a similar taste to a dry sherry.

Innes Fennell

The Classes of Wine

Italian wine produced since 1963 has now to conform to certain standards laid down by law.

D.O.C. — Denominazione di Origine Controllata
Roughly translated D.O.C. means 'typical of its type'. This mark means that the producer must reach a certain quality and minimum alcohol content. These wines do not have to be submitted to taste tests, so the system is not infallible.

Classico
This term guarantees that the wine is produced in the heart of the wine producing area. For example, a Chianti Classico will be far superior to an ordinary Chianti.

D.O.C.G. — Denominazione di Origine Controllata e Garantita
The status applied to the best quality wines. To be awarded this status, a wine must be submitted for taste tests.

Vino da Tavola
Strictly speaking, an ordinary table wine. Thousands of these are produced, all of varying qualities.

Riserva
A reserve applied to D.O.C. and D.O.C.G. wines after a specified period of ageing.

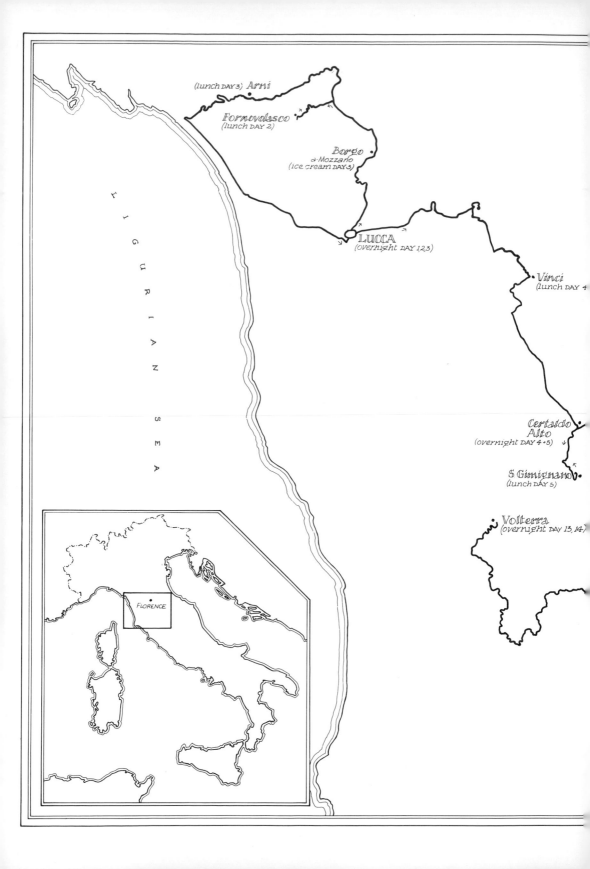

(lunch DAY 3) Arni •

Formovolasco •
(lunch DAY 2)

Borgo
a·Mozzano •
(ice cream DAY 3)

LIGURIAN SEA

LUCCA •
(overnight DAY 1,2,3)

• Vinci
(lunch DAY 4

Certaldo
Alto •
(overnight DAY 4+5)

S·Gimignano •
(lunch DAY 5)

• Volterra
(overnight DAY 13,14)

FLORENCE

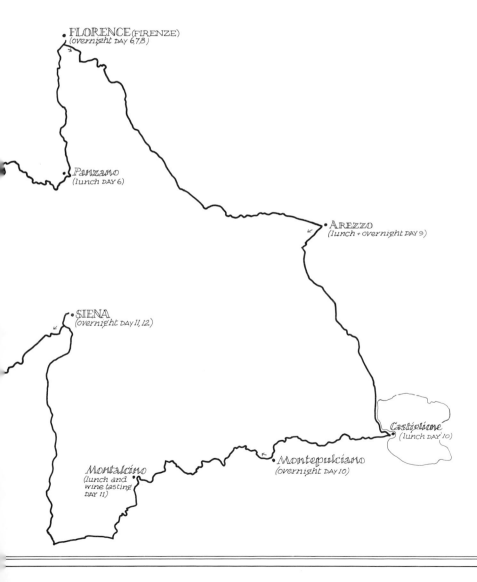

MAP OF TUSCANY
ITINERARY

N

FLORENCE (FIRENZE)
(overnight DAY 6,7,8)

Panzano
(lunch DAY 6)

AREZZO
(lunch + overnight DAY 9)

SIENA
(overnight DAY 11,12)

Castiglione
(lunch DAY 10)

Montepulciano
(overnight DAY 10)

Montalcino
(lunch and
wine tasting
DAY 11)

Handy Tips

HOW TO GET THERE
From Great Britain
By Air — the nearest international airport is at Pisa. Daily direct flights from Heathrow or Gatwick by Alitalia and Air Europe. Car hire facilities are, of course, available at Pisa, Aeroporto Pisa, Galileo Galilei (San Giusto) and prebooking is advisable.

By Rail — from London (or Paris), the Rome Express takes you direct to Pisa. The Inter-Rail Card permits persons under the age of 26 years, 30 days unlimited rail travel in participating countries. The Rail Europe Senior Card entitles the senior citizen to a discount on European rail journeys. Travel time: 22-24 hours approximately, car hire should be pre-booked.

By Car — ferry crossings Dover to Boulogne or Calais are the cheapest and quickest (1½ hours). Take the autoroutes via Paris to Lyons, then Chambery to Turin. Follow the A21 to Genoa and then the A12 to Pisa. Alternatively, off the autoroute from Calais/Boulogne to Soissons, Troyes, Dijon, Geneva, Chambery, Turin, Genoa and Pisa. We would suggest two overnight stops if you are driving to Pisa — perhaps in Dijon and then at Asti.

By Bus — from Victoria Coach Station in London (National Express) Eurolines. There are regular coach services from London to Florence. At Florence it is simple to hire a car or you could take the Autostrada all the way to Lucca.

From the U.S.A.
Direct flights are available to Rome from New York City, Philadelphia, Washington D.C., Boston and a few other major airports. To link up with your destination in Lucca, it is best to fly or train to Pisa and then hire a car. Alternatively, fly via London and on to Pisa.

WHEN TO GO
Any time from Easter to the end of October. July and August are extremely hot, especially in Florence which is considered to be Italy's hottest city.

Air Temperature	J.	F.	M.	A.	M.	J.	J.	A.	S.	O.	N.	D.
MAX. F	48	53	59	68	75	84	89	88	82	70	57	50
C	9	12	16	20	24	29	32	31	28	21	14	10
MIN F	35	36	40	46	53	59	62	61	59	52	43	37
C	2	2	5	8	12	15	17	17	15	11	6	3

Figures shown are approximate monthly averages for Florence.

Try to avoid travelling on, or just before, or after a bank holiday (see below). The worst time for traffic in Tuscany is the last Friday in July, when the Italians start their annual holiday.

PUBLIC HOLIDAYS IN ITALY

1st January	— Capodanno or Primo dell'Anno — New Year's Day
25th April	— Festa della Liberazione — Anniversary of the 1945 Liberation
1st May	— Festa del Lavoro — Labour Day
15th August	— Ferragosto — Assumption
1st November	— Ognissanti — All Saints' Day
8th December	— Immacolata Concezione — Immaculate Conception
25th December	— Natale — Christmas Day
26th December	— Santo Stefano — Saint Stephen's Day
Spring	— Lunedi di Pasqua — Easter Monday

In addition each town will celebrate the feast of its patron saint.

HOTELS
It is advisable to book hotels in advance. Hotels in Tuscany are generally open all year round.

CAMPING AND CARAVANNING
There are some wonderfully situated sites in Tuscany. These can get very crowded in Summer, so we would advise you to buy a copy of the *Touring Club*

Italiano (Campeggi e Villaggi Turistici in Italia). This is a directory of campsites in Italy and can be purchased in Italian bookshops. All sites have electricity, unlike dreary England. Small wooden bungalows are also available for rent at some camp sites.

SELF CATERING IN COTTAGES OR VILLAS
For information on staying in rural cottages or villas contact:

Perrymead Properties (overseas),   or Italien-Tours
55 Perrymead Street,   Vacanze Italiane,
London, SW6 3SN   22 Church Rise,
Tel: 01 736 4592   Forest Hill,
                                        London, SE23 2UD.
                                        Tel: 01 291 1450

or write to:
Main Office of Agriscambi
Foro Traiano
1A
00187
Rome
(Tel: 67 95 917)

Perrymead Properties (overseas) and Italien-Tours both offer villas, farm-houses and apartments in Tuscany and have been highly recommended to me by people who have used them in the past. If you vary my route slightly and prefer the freedom of self-catering to hotels, these accommodations will suit you admirably.

DRIVING
Driving on the right is usually no problem, the danger only comes when returning to the road from a car park, petrol station and, of course, at roundabouts. Traffic on major roads has right of way in Italy, but we found that the Italians tend to ignore the rules of the road completely. They drive impulsively and very fast, use their horns indiscriminately and expect visitors to do the same. Keep alert at all times and you will find, like us, that the Italians are really, despite appearances, good safe drivers. Seat belts are far from obligatory in Italy, but we advise you to wear them, because Tuscany is full of steep windy roads which can be very bumpy to say the least.

SPEED LIMITS
In Italy, maximum speeds are governed by engine capacity.

Engine Size	Main Roads	Motorways
Less than 600 cc	50 mph (80 kph)	56 mph (90 kph)
600/900 cc	56 mph (90 kph)	69 mph (110 kph)
900/1300 cc	62 mph (100 kph)	81 mph (130 kph)
More than 1300 cc	69 mph (110 kph)	87 mph (140 kph)

Town speed limits are signposted at the entrances of towns. Autostrada nearly all have periodic tolls and can be expensive on long journeys, but on the other hand, they save a lot of petrol, time and temper.

THE METRIC SYSTEM
Kilometers — for road distances, 8 km equals 5 miles, thus approximately:

Km:Miles	Km:Miles	Km:Miles
3:2	10:6	80: 50
4:2½	20:12	90: 56
5:3	30:18	100: 62
6:3½	40:25	125: 78
7:4	50:31	150: 94
8:5	60:37	175:110
9:5½	70:44	200:125

Litres — the British (Imperial) gallon is just over 4½ litres. The US Gallon about 3¾ litres, thus:

Litres	Brit. Gal.	US Gal.
5	1.1	1.3
10	2.2	2.7
15	3.3	4.0
20	4.4	5.3
30	6.7	8.0
40	8.8	10.6
50	11.1	13.3
100	22.2	26.7

When you get used to the price of motor fuel (benzina) in Italy, you may find it simplest to order it in multiples of 2000 lire. Petrol is considerably more expensive in Italy than the U.K. Petrol coupons may be obtained in the U.K. from the R.A.C. or A.A. motoring organisations or with the car registration documents at the Italian border. This will enable you to buy petrol at a slightly reduced rate depending upon foreign exchange. Credit cards are not taken at petrol stations in Tuscany. Watch out for lunch time, night and Sunday closings. The price of fuel which comes as regular (normale) and extra (super) is set by the Government.

TYRE PRESSURE
Measured in Kilograms per square centimetre. To convert lbs/sq.ins. to Kg/sq.cms. divide by 100 and multiply by 7, thus:

Lbs/sq.ins	Kg./sq.cms.
18	1.25
20	1.4
22	1.55
24	1.7
26	1.8
28	2.0
30	2.1
32	2.25
34	2.4

ROAD NUMBERS
We only found them on signs just outside main cities like Florence and Lucca. But fear not, signposting is good and our maps will see you through. A detailed map of Tuscany, however, would prove helpful.

BANKS
Banks are always shut on Saturdays and Sundays. Banking hours are 9 a.m. to 1.30 p.m. in the morning from Monday to Friday. Some banks open in the afternoon either between 2.30 p.m. and 3.30 p.m. or 3.00 p.m. and 4.00 p.m. This depends on the town and the day of the week, so it is much safer to go to the bank in the morning because there is nothing more irritating on holiday than to be short of money. When changing cheques/travellers' cheques or credit cards in Italy, always remember your passport.

SHOP OPENING TIMES
These vary according to a) type of shop, and b) size of town. In most places, shops are open on Saturday, but may be closed for part or all of Monday. They

are closed on Sunday. Normal opening times are from 9.00-12.30 p.m. and in the afternoon from 3.30/4.00 or 5.00 p.m. until 7.30 or 8.00 p.m. In tourist areas they may stay open even later.

Shops and banks are always closed on public holidays as already listed.

TELEPHONING

It is cheapest to use the modern coin boxes which are, in larger cities like Florence, scattered throughout the city and, in smaller cities, located in almost every bar. They are indicated by a yellow sign of a telephone dial outside the bar/cafe. Telephones take 'gettoni' (tokens of L.200) which can be bought at bars, hotels, post offices and tobacconists or, in the case of more modern ones, L.100 and L.200 coins. You can put plenty of money in before you start as it is returned if unused.

To make a call, insert up to six tokens and lift the receiver. After a short while you will hear a dialling tone — a series of regular dash-dash sounds. Then you can dial the number required. If no dialling tone appears put the receiver down and try again. Press the money back button to regain your 'gettoni'.

Calls within the same commune: Dial number required.

Calls to another commune: Dial the area code first, then the number required.

Calls to the U.K.: Dial 0044 for England, followed by the area code omitting the '0' and then the number you want.

Transatlantic calls: Consult hotel or post office (PTP — Posto Telefonico Publico) from where you can make collect calls.

TIPPING

A service charge is normally included within the price of restaurant meals in Italy (service included 'servizio e coperto' or just 'coperto') but in an expensive establishment you should leave 10% for courteous and efficient service.

It is polite to give a small tip to maids and hotel porters, about L.1,000 or 50 pence depending on exchange rates, and to give tour guides, taxi drivers and hairdressers 10% or 15%.

MONUMENTS AND MUSEUMS
Opening times and prices of admission have not been included in this book, as they are subject to change. All places mentioned are open to the public and will charge at least a couple of thousand lire for admission. Normally they will be open from 9 a.m. to 12 noon or 1.00 p.m. and then again from 2.00 p.m. or 3.00 p.m. to about 5.00 p.m. Check in major cities, i.e. Florence, as some do not open in the afternoon at all.

CONSULATE
The United Kingdom Consulate is situated in Florence:
U.K. Consulate,
Lungarno Corsini 2,
Florence.
Tel. No. (055) 284133

We hope you will not need to use the Consulate, but in the case of an emergency, it is the best place to go.

KEY TO ITINERARY
Rating are for prices/room/night and for meals.

★★   reasonable
★★★   average
★★★★   expensive
★★★★★   very expensive

Lunch and dinner are distinguished by the following symbols:

 Lunch    *Dinner*

The Itinerary

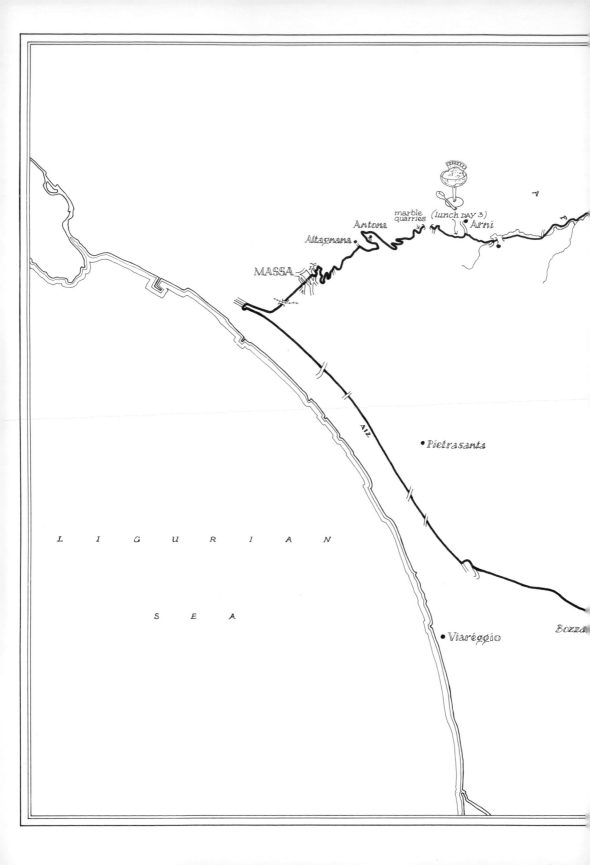

marble
quarries

(lunch DAY 3)

Antona

Altagnana

MASSA

Arni

• Pietrasanta

A12

L I G U R I A N

S E A

• Viaréggio

Bozza

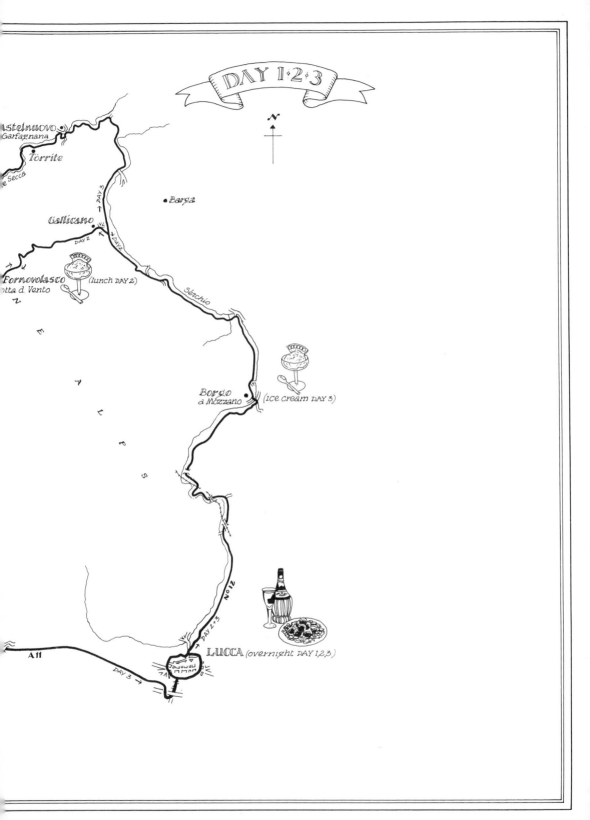

DAY 1·2·3

N

Castelnuovo
di Garfagnana

Torrite

e Secca

• Barga

← DAY 3

Gallicano

DAY 2

Fornovolasco

otta d. Vento

(lunch DAY 2)

Senchio

E
A
L
P
S

Borgo
a Mozzano

(ice cream DAY 3)

N° 12

DAY 2+3

A 11

DAY 3

LUCCA (overnight DAY 1,2,3)

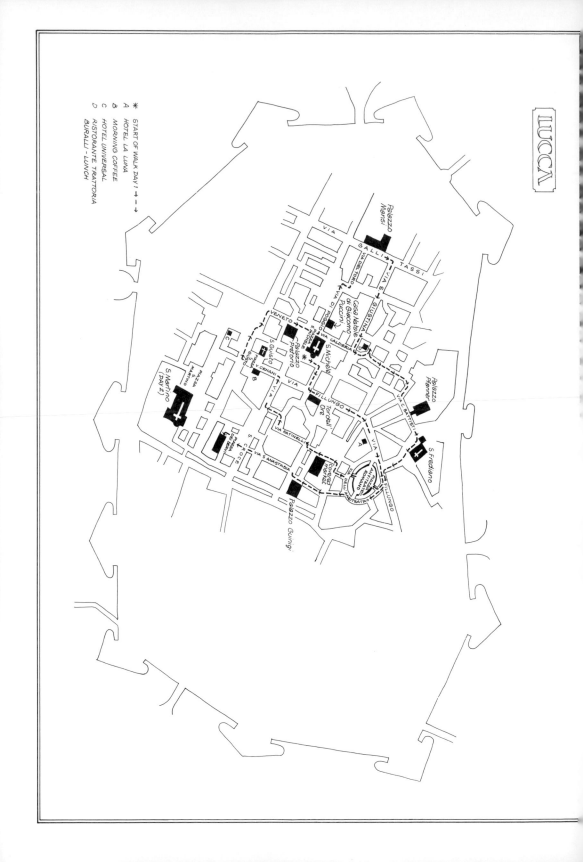

LUCCA

* START OF WALK DAY 1 → → →
A HOTEL LA LUNA
B MORNING COFFEE
C HOTEL UNIVERSAL
D RISTORANTE TRATTORIA
   BURALLI - LUNCH

The Journey Begins

DAY 1

Arrive Lucca

Lucca is a fascinating medieval citadel encased by its sixteenth-century tree-lined walls only a short distance from tourist-filled Pisa.

The city flourished in the Middle Ages when it was a banking and merchant centre and was famous for beautiful silk. In 1369, it bought its independence from Pisa for 100,000 florins and has prospered ever since. Today, it is noted for wines, textiles, flowers and the very best olive oil in the world.

Within its walls, the city is rich in art and architecture. There are many very narrow streets in which to wander, quiet secluded squares in which to reflect and so, it is from here, a city Innes and I particularly liked, that your journey will begin.

Dinner and overnight at the Hotel la Luna, Lucca.

Lucca

After breakfast in your hotel, we suggest you take a promenade around the city streets.

Piazza San Michele

The Piazza San Michele stands on the site of the original Roman forum, so it is not surprising to find that the heavily carved Pisan/Lucchese church which dominates this square is called La Chiesa di San Michele in Foro (the Church of St Michael in the Forum). Construction of the church began in the 12th century and continued over several different periods, as its varied architecture betrays. A huge bronze statue of the Archangel Michael surmounts the truly remarkable facade, keeping watch over the slim columns above which animals are depicted in geometrical designs. In the 19th century, the facade was restored and numerous busts, including those of Garibaldi, Napoleon III and Cavour were added.

The interior of this church is somewhat plain and disappointing after the elegant and stunning facade, but in the north transept there is a delicate, brightly coloured painting of the four saints — Sebastian, Roch, Jerome and Helen — by Filippo Lippi.

Also to be seen in the square is the Palazzo Pretorio, dating from the late 15th century, a fine example of renaissance architecture; and the monument and statue to Francesco Burlamacchi by Ulisse Cambi, which was brought here in 1863.

The Via Fillungo, which has many interesting shop facades, takes you to the Torre dell'ore, clock tower, called in ancient times the 'Torre della Lite', tower of quarrels, for the inhabitants used to hurl boulders from these towers at their enemies. It is believed that in the Middle Ages, Lucca boasted over 130 of these towers, imagine the commotion. This is the only one that survives today. The clock has reliably ticked off the hours for the public of Lucca since 1471.

The Via Fillungo takes you on to the Piazza Amfiteatro Romano. This elliptical shaped piazza has been built on the site of an ancient Roman amphitheatre of the first and second century A.D. The buildings, which assume the shape of the original theatre that we see today, were altered around 1830 by the urban architect, Lorenzo Nottolini. He successfully managed to form arches on street level, whilst retaining the higgledy-piggledly roof shape. Unfortunately, the piazza has fallen into disrepair, it is hoped that one day it will be restored to its former glory.

Behind the square is Lucca's wonderful covered market. A stroll around all its varied stalls full of every type of fruit, vegetable, bread, meat and charcuterie available in Tuscany, is a refreshing relief from ancient history. You may even like to buy some local bread, cheese and salami here for a picnic lunch on the battlements.

We suggest you take a coffee break in the Piazza San Giusto.

The Piazza San Giusto is somewhat spoilt by a modern building known by the Lucchese as 'Il Palazzaccio' (ugly building), for this suffocates the small 12th-century Chiesa di San Giusto, which has quite exquisite carvings around its main doorway.

Refreshed after coffee, take a walk across the Piazza Napoleone to Via di Poggia, where you will find the house where Giacomo Puccini was born in 1858. It is now a small museum and houses many of Puccini's manuscripts, documents and mementos, including the 'Turandot' piano and the maestro's overcoat, in beautiful 15th-century rooms.

Palazzo Mansi

This palace, which was built at the end of the 16th century and the beginning of the 17th century, has recently become state property and houses, amongst other things, Lucca's National Picture Gallery containing mainly paintings donated to the town in 1847 by Granduca Leopoldi II of Tuscany, and those donated in 1861 by Guardoroba Mediceo.

You will note one of the most important works of Pontorno, circa 1525, a portrait of the young Allessandro de Medici, and a painting on wood — *The Continence of Scipio* — by Domenico Beccafumi (14th century). Our personal favourite was the central painting in the first picture gallery, *La Madona Appare a San Giacinto*, by Jacopo Ligozzi (1547-1627).

Leading off the fresco-covered ballroom (frescoes by Gioseffo dal Sole, 17th century) are three magnificent drawing rooms, hung with well-preserved Brussels tapestries woven on drawings by Joustus Egmont in 1665, which lead to the Camera degli Sposi — the bridal chamber — the pièce de résistance of this museum.

The walls are covered with mirrors, stuccoes (cement moulded into architectural decorations) and the precious silks for which Lucca is famous. The alcove, which holds the impressive canopied matrimonial bed, is separated by an elaborate baroque arch of gilded wood supported by four oriental figures adorned with fruits.

Lunch at Trattoria Da 'Leo' Dei F.LLI.

After lunch, and while you are probably wondering how you are going to fit into your clothes when you return home, we suggest that the most appropriate place to visit is the Palazzo Pfanner.

Palazzo Pfanner

This palace which now houses some very beautiful Lucchese costumes from the 18th and 19th centuries, was built about 1667 (architect as yet unidentified). The facade style is late 16th century, but the staircase and loggia show definite Baroque influence. The staircase goes to the suite of rooms on the main floor which is now the Costume Museum. These rooms are decorated with 'false perspective' by Pietro Scrosini (early 18th century).

The loggia invites you out into a charming 18th-century Italian garden, undoubtedly designed by Filippo Juvarra, famous in Lucca at that time. The path to the lemon-house is lined with statues representing the seasons, months of the year and gods, to such effect that one could imagine Romans in togas here, lounging around the octagonal pool, with a backcloth of Lucca's old tree-lined avenues, which surround the battlements. A delightful scene.

Close by, in the Piazza San Frediano, is the Chiesa San Frediano.

Chiesa San Frediano

After the Cathedral (see p. 70) this is probably Lucca's most impressive church with a huge dazzling gold mosaic on its upper facade which has been tastefully restored.

It is said that the original church which stood here was founded by the Irish Bishop Frediano in 1112, and that his remains are buried under the present high altar.

At the beginning of the twelfth century, the church was completely rebuilt. The font was dramatically heightened in the 13th century and the outstanding Byzantine mosaic you see today was placed on the facade.

The interior is fairly plain but it contains a wonderful font, the mummified remains of Santa Zita (the object of various legends and ceremonies), and a fresco depicting the removal of the Volto Sancto from Luni to Lucca in the chapel of St Augustine. (Note: The Volto Sancto is now in the Cathedral.)

The 12th-century font was taken apart in the 18th century, however, it was luckily kept in good order and was carefully reassembled in 1959 from a drawing held in Lucca's archives.

This extraordinary piece of carving has a circular base with a large inner basin, above which is a smaller basin supported by a pillar and crowned by an ornamental dome resting on delicate columns. The sculptural decoration is extremely complex and beautiful and is believed to have been the work of three different people, two of whom were responsible for the highly intricate base. The first of these, of Lombard origin but unidentified for certain, carved with superb craftsmanship some stories of Moses. The most striking is *The Journey across the Red Sea*; the soldiers resemble medieval knights.

To the second — Maestro Roberto — we owe *The Good Shepherd* and the *Six Prophets*. His work can be clearly distinguished by his strong Byzantine style. The third artist, again unknown, but of definite Tuscan classical origin, sculpted the fine work on the upper basin and dome. He depicts the apostles on the lid, and the months of the year beneath. Even though it was probably slightly defaced during its reassembly, the font remains a wonderful sculpture worthy of detailed study.

The remains of Santa Zita are kept in the adjoining chapel, she died in 1278. There is an associated legend which goes thus.

It says that she was a servant of the Fatinelli family (nobles at that time), and that one day as she was hiding some bread to give to the poor in her apron, her master surprised her and asked "What are you hiding?" She replied, "Roses and flowers, master", and behold when she revealed the contents of her apron, the bread had miraculously changed into flowers.

On the 26th April each year, the streets around this church are transformed with flowers, the mummified body is placed in the centre of the church and the townspeople come to stroke and kiss its withered limbs in deathly silence.

A very strange custom indeed.

The Chapel of St Augustine is situated in the left aisle, near the side entrance, and is completely covered by frescoes painted by the Bolognese, Amico Aspertini from 1508-1509 (some are unfortunately damaged). The frescoes represent *The Miraculous Diversion of the River Serchio by Frediano Himself*; a *Nativity*; *The Christening of Saint Augustine by St Ambrogio*; and *The Legend of the Movement of the Volto Sancto from Luni to Lucca*, the legend is recounted on p. 71. Tradition has it that once the Volto Sancto had arrived in Lucca it was placed here first, before its relocation in the Cathedral where it stands today.

En route to the best view over Lucca, why not stop and treat yourself to a thirst quenching and delicious Italian 'gelati'.

The Palazzo Guinigi and its unusual tower were constructed at the end of the 14th century completely from bricks, and are the last and best surviving examples of the traditional Roman/Gothic merchants' houses of Lucca.

The tower is open to the public, and it is well worth climbing its 231 steps to the top to see centuries old holm-oaks (evergreen oaks) and the most spectacular panorama of Lucca, and the surrounding countryside. The palazzo will be undergoing renovation and so will one day soon be open too.

Before you return to your hotel to get ready for dinner take a walk via the Piazza dei Servi, for tucked away in the corner you will discover the Chiesa di san Maria dei Servi. A delightful 13th-century church which from the outside looks very plain, but it is quite beautiful within.

Overnight at the Hotel la Luna, Lucca.

If you are not feeling too well fed or just exhausted after today, I can recommend an evening stroll around the 16th/17th century city walls, from where you can experience at every step a different view of Lucca's charms.

Trattoria Da 'Leo' Dei F.lli
Buralli
Via Tegrimi 1
Lucca
Tel: 42236

Restaurant closed Sunday evening and all day Monday.

Hotel La Luna
Via Fillungo
Corte Compagni 12
Lucca 55100
Tel: 43634/5

A family-run hotel in the heart of old Lucca. This would be our choice, for it is small and friendly and has a private car park. Advance booking essential.

Open all year.
Rooms:	All rooms have private bathrooms
Facilities:	Bar, lounge, T.V., private car park
Credit Cards:	Diners, Visa, American Express
Food:	No restaurant/breakfast available
Rating:	★★

Hotel Universo
Piazza Puccini 1
Piazza Napoleone
Lucca 55100
Tel: 43678
Telex: 621840 LUSALA

An impressive hotel opposite the opera house. Very central and close to plenty of good restaurants. Advance booking essential.

Open all year.	
Rooms:	Most have private bathrooms.
Facilities:	Lift, T.V., restaurant and terrace
Credit Crads:	Hotel — Visa
	Restaurant — American Express and Visa
Food:	Adequate, but as I have already mentioned hotel food can be average. Eat out if possible.
Rating:	★★★

DAY 2

Lucca – Fornovolasco – Lucca

After visiting Lucca's magnificent Cathedral, today's excursion includes lunch in the picturesque mountain village of Fornovolasco, and an optional tour of the Grotta del Vento, the Wind Caves. Full of stalagmites and stalactites, they descend into the Apuane Alps for over two miles.

Travel Information
Total Mileage: approx. 50 miles

Palazzo Pfanner, Lucca

Breakfast at Hotel la Luna.

Before leaving for Fornovolasco, take a little time to view Lucca's Cathedral.

Duomo San Martino

Despite the long period of time that was involved in its construction, and indeed many alterations, this great Cathedral still holds a harmonious spirit. It was originally founded in the 6th century, and rebuilt by Bishop Anselmo de Baggio, who became Pope Alexander II. By 1070, however, very little of the original structure still stood.

The present Cathedral was begun in the 12th century and was not finished until the latter part of the 15th century.

The asymmetrical facade, which appears to lean against the Romanesque Bell Tower, is like so many others, influenced by the Cathedral at Pisa. It is the oldest part and the most architecturally impressive, being carved with fantastic animals on or above slender columns, some of which are made of green marble. You will probably notice that it looks unfinished, this is because it lacks the last tier and a Tympanum; if it had been completed it would have most likely resembled the facade of La Chiesa di San Michele (p. 62).

It is impossible to identify for certain the artists involved in the marvellous decorations on the Atrium, but they would most definitely have included Maestro Lombardo and Guido Bigarelli.

The Tympanums above the three doorways show, from left to right, *The Descent from the Cross*; *The Ascension*; and the *Martyrdom of St Regolo*. Between the doorways are bas-reliefs showing episodes of the life of St Martin and representations of the months of the year.

The interior of the Cathedral was remodelled, work began in 1372 and took almost a whole century. It has slender pillars and a glorious deep blue ceiling studded with gold stars.

In the centre of the nave stands the celebrated 'Tempietto', (Matteo Civitali, 1484), an octagonal gilded cage which protects the life-sized crucifix — the Volto Sancto. Christ gazes wearily down from the cross. Legend has it that it was engraved out of a Lebanese cedar tree by Nicodemus in the 7th or 8th century and kept hidden for centuries against persecution. Then one day it was placed on a boat and sent to sea. Miraculously the relic was left unharmed by the terrors of the Mediterranean and eventually drifted ashore at Luni. At once, the residents of Luni, together with those of Lucca, claimed possession, so to leave the choice of its final seat to divine justice, it was put on an ox-drawn cart. The oxen immediately started off for Lucca where the Volto Sancto has remained ever since.

Leave Lucca to the north, taking the No 12 (S), which is signposted to Abertone and Modena. Proceed following signs to Borgo a Mozzano/Barga.

A short distance after Borga a Mozzano bear left onto the road to Castelnuovo di Garf. Then turn left to Gallicano and Fornovolasco. The road will become posted with yellow signs to the Grotta del Vento, it is very narrow and cut into the steep rocks of the forested gorge. Take it carefully and don't forget to hoot at bends.

Fornovolasco

The beautiful village of Fornovolasco is even today unknown to most foreign tourists. Water rushes between its steep narrow streets, and alleys wind through a maze of tunnels. The air here is fresh and the water pure from the mountain streams. It reminded us, in a way, of an idyllic filmset.

Lunch at the Ristorante La Buca, Fornovolasco.

Here you can relax over a simple lunch of antipasti and fresh trout whilst listening to the rushing water of the stream beside, and taking in the awe-inspiring view of the mountains.

After lunch do drive up to the caves and take a guided tour.

The Grotta del Vento

These extraordinary caves are situated in one of the most picturesque zones of the Apuane Alps, and are considered to be of major scientific interest. A guided tour through the cave complex is highly recommended. The numerous cave tours of different lengths, are available daily from April-September, however in high season it is wisest to book in advance at the Head Office, 'Grotta del Vento', 55020 Fornovolasco tel: 0583/763084-763068. You can book from your hotel.

Return to Lucca.

USEFUL INFORMATION: LUCCA

Tourist Office:	Via Vittorio Veneto 40,
E.P.T. *	off P. Napoleone,
	Tel: 43639
	Open: Mon.-Sat. 9-12 and
	3.30-6.30
Population:	approximately 91,000
Altitude:	19 m (62 ft)
Telephone Code:	0583
Postal Code:	55100
Entertainment:	1) The Estate Musicale Lucchese — a musical calendar from July to September. 2) The Festival di Marlia — features operas of Giacomo Puccini late July, August and September. 3) Settembre Lucchese — a festival of artistic, athletic and folklore presentations, in September.

* E.P.T. = Ente Provinciale per il Turismo (Tourist office)

From Mountains to Marvels

DAY 3

Lucca–Massa–Lucca

A drive through Tuscany's magnificent marble mountains from where Michaelangelo obtained the white marble for his masterpiece, 'David'.

Travel Information
Total Mileage: approx. 90 miles

Lucca to Castelnuovo di Garfagnana — 31 miles, about 1 hour
Castelnuovo di Garf. to Ristorante Il Castellacio for lunch — approx. 16 miles, 40 mins
Il Castellacio to Massa, allowing plenty of time to view the marble quarries — approx. 14 miles, about 1½ hours
Massa to Lucca via Autostrada A11/12 — approx. 30 miles, about 30 mins.

Travels in Tuscany

Breakfast at Lucca.

Leave Lucca and drive north via Borgo a Mozzano to Castelnuovo di Garfagnana. When we went, we decided to stop at Borgo a Mozzano outside the café Il Pescatore, just beside the bridge, and treat ourselves to a delicious mixed gelati topped with liqueur cherries.

Drive on to Castelnuovo di Garf. Now follow the signs to Fortei di Marmi. This road will take you via Torrite, through a narrow gorge, past a small dam which produces hydro-electric power, and on to Arni. You will be able to admire beautiful mountain peaks with sheer rock faces along the way, together with the chestnut covered, gloriously green, lower slopes which border the road.

Just past the signpost, which indicates that you have arrived at Arni, turn sharp left. This is the road to Massa, but may not be signposted. Beware! This unmade road climbs steeply up to a tunnel. Proceed through the tunnel and on your right you will see the restaurant Il Castellacio. This is where you should stop for lunch. It doesn't look much from the outside, but within, it is welcoming, clean, and has good loos! and above all, it is surrounded by marble quarries. What more could you want?

After lunch continue along this quite horrifically surfaced road and bear left into another tunnel. (Note: the road may be re-surfaced by now.)

On a good afternoon the view of the quarries at the end of this tunnel is breathtaking. Walls of white marble glisten in the sunlight. We found it a magnificent sight.

It is incredible to think that marble has been quarried here for over 2000 years. In earlier times, one can imagine the difficulties that had to be overcome in the quarrying of these large blocks, let alone in transporting them down to the docks for export. Frequently of course, men lost their lives, as heavy blocks would break loose and crush them at their work. Today the marble is now carried down to the ports by lorry, from where it is shipped all over the world.

From here the road (now fully surfaced) runs down via a series of tunnels and steep hair-pin bends towards Massa. There are some spectacular views from this road which passes through some pretty villages too. The hillside villages of Antonna and Altagnana look as though they are hugging the rocks for fear of falling from their perch.

On the approach to Massa, look to the west, for in the distance you will be able to see the sea. Massa itself is not a particularly pleasant town and we suggest that you head for the Autostrada A11/12 to return to Lucca, to give the driver a well-deserved rest from eye-straining mountain roads.

Dinner and overnight at Lucca.

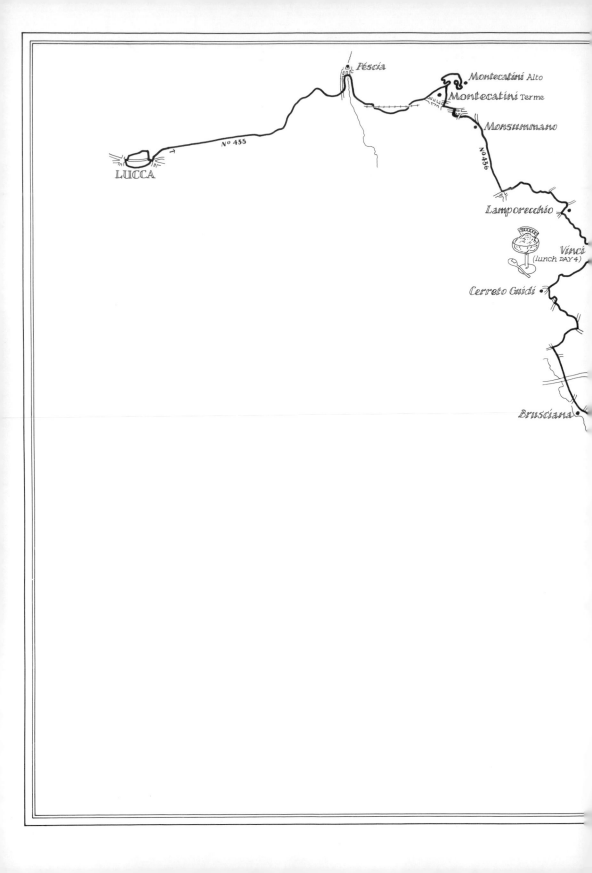

N

• Fiésole

FLORENCE
(FIRENZE)
(overnight DAY 6,7,8)

No 222

• Greve

-poli

• Castelfiorentino

No 429

Tavarnelle
V. di Pesa

Morrocco

Panzano
(lunch DAY 6)

Certaldo (overnight DAY 4,5)
Alto

S. Donato

Sicelle

• Pieve
di Panzano

Sciano

No 2

Piazza

No 222

S. Gimignano
(lunch DAY 5)

Restaurant — Certaldo Alto

DAY 4

Lucca to Certaldo Alto

Today's trip takes you to Vinci, where Leonardo was born, and then on through a varied landscape to Certaldo Alto, the town which was once the seat of the Counts Alberti and became Florentine in 1293.

Travel Information
Total Mileage: approx. 60 miles

Lucca to Vinci: 35.7 miles, about 2 hours including coffee
Vinci to Certaldo Alto: 24 miles, about 1 hour

Travels in Tuscany

Breakfast at Lucca.

Leave Lucca eastwards on the No 435 signposted to Pistoia. Then follow signs to Montecatini. At Montecatini turn left and left again to Montecatini Alto, which is situated about 10 minutes up a winding road on the top of an olive covered hillside.

Montecatini Alto

Drive around the village until you see the sign 'Ristorante Apogeo'. Here you can park under the trees and walk into the central square. The old world hill-top village of Montecatini Alto, also known as Montecatini Val di Nievole, is situated at an altitude of 951 ft. From its walls there are wonderful views of the olive groves which cover the hillside and the famous thermal spa town below, which the Italian aristocracy have frequented since Roman times.

In the picturesque Piazza Guiseppe Giusto there are several open air cafes/restaurants, where you can sit and savour a rather expensive coffee. Out of season this is truly a delightful setting.

Montecatini Alto can also be reached by a funicular railway from Viale Diaz in Montecatini Terme below.

Refreshed after coffee, drive back down to Montecatini Terme, which is an expensive high class resort reminiscent of Monaco, and take the road signposted to Monsummano. (This road may also be signposted to Pistoia and Firenze.)

At Monsummano turn right at the traffic lights onto the No 436 signposted to Fucecchio. Continue for about 4 miles, and then turn left signposted to Larciano. After a mile the road will be signposted to Vinci; follow this road through Lamporecchio and then turn left along Via Leonardo da Vinci to Vinci itself. On reaching Vinci stop for a light lunch at the Albergo Ristorante Gina, which you will spot on your right.

After lunch drive up into Vinci (turn left at the traffic lights signposted to Casa Natale di Leonardo), follow signs to Centro and Museum. Park and walk.

Vinci

This little medieval town lies in fertile countryside on the south western slope of Monte Albano. It is, of course, the town of the great artist, architect, inventor, astronomer . . . Leonardo. It is not surprising then to find that the beautifully restored castle is now the Museo Vinciano devoted to Leonardo da Vinci's works. It is an extremely interesting museum containing models based on Leonardo's drawings, and has full descriptions in English.

Just one mile to the north on the Anchiano road, approached through olive groves, is the country house where Leonardo was born in 1452.

Leave Vinci, taking the road to Cerreto which passes through undulating hills covered with neat vineyards. After 3 miles turn left signed Empoli/Firenze and after a short distance left again signed Empoli. It is worth stopping occasionally to view the scenery.

After another 5½ miles change onto the Siena road, and then keep towards Siena on the No 429. Here the countryside changes from the sublime to the ridiculous, for on the last lap of your way to Certaldo you will run through an industrial dump which ruins the Tuscan landscape.

In Certaldo turn left, right and left again following the signs to Certaldo Alto. The rough road which leads to the oasis where you will spend the next 2 nights, is somewhat uninviting, but persevere, it really is worth it.

Certaldo Alto

This old medieval city, built in red brick, produces some excellent wines, but is most famous for its association with Giovanni Boccaccio, author of the *Decameron*, who spent the last years of his life here.

Dinner and overnight at the hotel Il Castello, Certaldo Alto.

Albergo Ristorante Gina
Via Lamporecchiana
Vinci

This restaurant is a convenient venue to stop for lunch. The menu is extremely extensive and each dish is explained in English. We would however, suggest a light lunch, for the hotel/restaurant in which you will stay in Certaldo Alto is quite excellent.

Hotel Il Castello
Via B. Della Rena 6
50052 Certaldo Alto
Firenze
Tel: (0571) 668250

The hotel Il Castello is an adorable little family-run hotel, with a terrace which can only be described as a floral oasis, and a very good restaurant. The bedrooms are attractive and clean, and some have private bathrooms. Advance booking is definitely recommended here.

Credit Cards:	Amex and Visa from 1988
Food:	Try Zuppa (see p. 145), Antipasta Misto, and Saltimbocca alla Romana (see p. 151)
Wine:	the local red and house white are both of good quality
Rating:	★★

Hotel Osteria del Vicario
Certaldo Alto
Firenze
Tel: (0571) 668228

A hotel with history, for it was once an old monastery. A family-run hotel where the chef/owner is of Tuscan origin and specialises in regional cuisine. All rooms have private bathrooms.

Credit Cards:	Visa, Diners, Amex
Food/Wine:	The owners recommendations for the day are always reliable and interesting. The menu changes very regularly.

Closed:	Mid January to mid March. Booking recommended. Note: The restaurant is closed to the general public on Wednesdays.
Facilities:	Small swimming pool and pretty terrace
Rating:	★★

USEFUL INFORMATION: CERTALDO ALTO

Tourist Office:	Situated in the main street, excellent service
Altitude:	130 metres (425 ft)
Population:	Including Certaldo Terme about 16,000

San Gimignano

Medieval Still Today

DAY 5

Day trip to San Gimignano

Based at Certaldo Alto, today your day will be spent in San Gimignano. Stroll along the narrow streets lined with Gothic-Romanesque palaces, enjoy lunch at the Ristorante La Stella, view the Cathedral, and climb the 220 steps to the top of the 'Big Tower'.

Travel Information
Total Mileage: 20 miles

Travels in Tuscany

Breakfast at Certaldo Alto.

You will find that there is a short made-up road to take you down from Certaldo Alto to the lower town. Turn right at the bottom, then left through the town following signs to San Gimignano.

San Gimignano

A word of caution — you will naturally wish to park your car before exploring Gimignano on foot. Do not park in the public warden-controlled carparks, these are terrifically overpriced. We found free places away from the main gates.

San Gimignano, whether known as 'The town of the beautiful towers' or 'The Manhattan of the Middle Ages', is a magnificent sight. It is situated on a ridge above the Elsa valley, surrounded by walls and dominated by 13 towers (there were originally 72). We know, from tombs and burial objects which have been discovered near the town, that it was Etruscan in origin, but its present name comes from St Geminianus the 4th-century Bishop of Modena, who died in AD 347. However, the town gained its historical fame in the Middle Ages when, being on a major route into Rome, it was able to secure great prosperity from profitable trade, notably from saffron.

In the 12th century San Gimignano declared itself a free community (up until this time it was governed from Volterra), and in the 13th century it suffered many bloody internal battles between Guelph and Ghibelline families. The towers built at this time were designed as keeps and from these towers the nobles hurled ammunition at their rivals, as in Lucca. In 1353 the town finally submitted to the power of Florence.

The Cathedral stands in the Piazza del Duomo. When we were there local musicians were playing enchanting medieval music and pavement artists were decorating the streets with drawings.

Collegiata S. Maria Assunta

Although this church is generally known as a cathedral it shouldn't be, since San Gimignano has never been the seat of a Bishop. This Romanesque church probably dates back to the 12th century; in 1466 it was transformed into a Latin cross plan by Giuliano da Maiano; and the facade was restored in 1818. Inside, the walls are covered with frescoes. I don't think I've ever seen anything quite so amazing. The frescoes are 14th- and 15th-century and depict scenes from the Old Testament (on the north/left aisle) and stories from the New Testament (on the south/right aisle). The Old Testament scenes were painted by the Sienese artist Bartola Battilori (c. 1330-1410) and were inspired by the works of Simone Martini and Lorenzetti. The New Testament stories, were executed by the artist Barna, who according to Vasari died in 1381 after falling off the scaffolding on which he was working, and were finished by his nephew Giovani di Asciano.

The inside of the facade shows *The Last Judgement, Heaven and Hell* by Taddeo di Bartolo (1393); and the *Martyrdom of St Sebastian* by Benozzo Gozzoli (1405). At the far end of the south aisle is the Chapel of Santa Fina. This local saint was known as the saint of wallflowers, for it is said that these flowers sprang up in her coffin and on the town's towers on her dying day. The chapel itself was built by Giuliano da Maiano in 1468.

Note — As in many of Italy's churches there are slot machines to turn on the lights. A few hundred lire are necessary.

Palazzo del Popolo — closed Mondays

This was the seat of the government from the end of the 13th century and is still today the Town Hall. It houses San Gimignano's municipal Art Gallery and contains a number of religious works of art, notably an *Annunciation* by Filippino Lippi (1483).

The Palace is dominated by its 117 ft tall square tower. It really is worth climbing the 220 steps to the top, for the views over the brown roof tops and the Tuscan countryside are breathtaking. The Palace is closed Mondays.

You may also wish to visit the Museum of Sacred Art and the Etruscan museum. The former adjoins the Collegiate church and contains 14th- and 15th-century sculpture and sacred vestments; the latter has a fine collection of urns, coins and bronzes discovered during excavations in the immediate area; or you may just wish to wander around the narrow streets. Whichever is your choice, be sure to buy or try San Gimignano's famous white wine 'Vernaccia'.

Drive back to your hotel in Certaldo Alto for dinner and overnight accommodation.

Ristorante La Stella
Via S. Matteo 77
53037 San Gimignano
Siena
Tel: (0577) 940444

The chef of this pleasant little restaurant is Anna Maria Masini, she has a lively interest in tasty genuine recipes. The ambiance here is both Italian and friendly.

Try some of her specialities, they include:
> *Penne alla Stella* — Short quill shaped pasta with a cream, tomato and mushroom sauce.
> *Cinghiale in Salmi* — Wild Boar in a tomato sauce with red wine and various fresh herbs.
> *Stracatto al Chianti* — Braised beef cooked in local red wine with a delicious sauce (cook's secret).
> *Cantuccini con Vin Santo* — Small biscuits with almonds, served with dessert wine.

Credit Cards:	Visa, Amex
Closed:	Wednesdays, and for one month a year, usually January.

If you have been unlucky in booking an hotel in Certaldo Alto here are two alternatives from which to choose.

Hotel La Cisterna
Piazza Cisterna
53037 San Gimignano
Siena
Tel: (0577) 940328

Lovely hotel with magnificent views over the Val d'Elsa.

Restaurant: good
Rating: ★★★

Hotel Leon Bianco
Piazza Cisterna
53037 San Gimignano
Siena
Tel: (0577) 941294

Well-decorated hotel with 21 bedrooms all with bathrooms. The hotel has the benefit of a garage.

Rating: ★★★

USEFUL INFORMATION — SAN GIMIGNANO

Tourist Office:	Piazza Duomo
Altitude:	332 metres (1089 ft)
Population:	7521
Facilities:	Camping and hotels

View to Mountains from Barga

DAY 6

From Certaldo Alto to Florence (Firenze)

A drive through the Chianti hills to the great art city. A wonderful experience at any time.

Travel Information
Total Mileage: approx. 45 miles
Certaldo Alto to Panzano — approx. 23 miles, about 1½ hours.
Panzano to Florence — approx. 22 miles, about 1 hour.

Breakfast at Certaldo Alto.

After a light breakfast, because lunch should be taken at a leisurely pace today, leave Certaldo Alto.

Drive down to the main road No 429 by the short route. Turn left to Montesperto/S. Casciano/Fiano and then after only ¾ mile turn right signposted to Bagnano/Sciano/Barberino/Petrognano.

As you climb up, on this winding road, surrounded by grape vines and olive groves, stop and look back at Certaldo Alto, for this small citadel can be seen well from here.

After a further 5¾ miles turn left and follow the Barberino road until you hit the SS2 to Firenze (Florence). Bear left onto this road and continue through Tavernelle Val di Pesa. Turn right signposted San Donato/Siena/Sambuca/Strada de Vino Chianti Classico.

Follow the signs to San Donato, crossing over the Siena/Firenze superstrada, drive on until you see the sign for Sicelle. Turn left onto this road. Never fear if it is still just gravel for it does eventually become tarmac. It is a pretty road through hills crowned with the vines which produce the famous Chianti Classico.

After about a further 4 miles you will reach the SS222. Turn left onto this road towards Firenze. Arrive at Panzano and turn left to the centre of the village.

Panzano

Panzano lies in the heart of Chianti Classico. It was a Florentine border fortress until the castle was razed to the ground by the Ghibellines in 1260. This event is still commemorated every April.

The Romanesque parish church dominates this village from where there are wonderful views over Chianti and the Pesa valley.

Lunch should be taken on the terrace overlooking the vineyards at the Ristorante Il Vescovino.

After lunch return to the SS222 and drive to Florence.

Dinner and hotel accommodation in Florence.

Il Vescovino
Ristorante — American bar
Panzano
Chianti
Firenze

A restaurant with a fantastic view and food to match. Good service and the added benefit of English-speaking staff.

Why not try the famous Bistecca alla Fiorentina, washed down with a good full-bodied red Chianti Classico?

Hotel Bernini
Piazza San Firenze 29
50122 Firenze
Tel: (055) 278621
Telex: 573616

Located just behind the Palazzo Vecchio, this is a new hotel in an attractive setting right in the heart of the historical centre.

Credit Cards:	Yes
Open:	All year — high season 1 April to 16 November
Facilities:	Snack bar, bar, air conditioning, radio and TV, garage
Rooms:	90, all with private facilities
Rating:	★★★★★

Hotel Calzaiuoli
Via Calzaiuoli 6
50122 Firenze
Tel: (055) 212456/7/8
Telex: 58589

A hotel providing good bed and breakfast accommodation, located in the
only pedestrian street of the city, between the Cathedral and Piazza
Signoria.

Credit Cards:	Yes
Facilities:	Telephones in all bedrooms
Rooms:	44, all with private facilities
Rating:	★★★★

USEFUL INFORMATION — FLORENCE

Altitude:	50 metres (165 ft)
Population:	460,000
Festivals:	7th September — The night Festival of the Lanterns — RIFICOLONI April-May — International craft exhibition Easter Sunday is celebrated in the Piazza del Duomo
Tourist Office:	Via A. Manzoni 16 Tel: 247 81 41
Main line station:	Santa Maria Novella Station (nr centre of town) Trains direct to Pisa Airport, Rome Small Tourist Office, useful for maps etc.
Facilities:	*Swimming pool*, Bellariva, Lungarno Columbo 2 (Tel: 6775 21) *Car Rental*, Hertz, Via Fininguerra 11, (Tel: 29 45 78). *Police* (for foreigners), Via Zara 2, (Tel: 497 71) 9am-2pm. *Emergency calls:* Dial 113.

A Cultural Experience

DAY 7 and DAY 8

Florence — as there is so much to see and enjoy in the city, determining the length of your stay here must be a matter of your personal taste. Within the confines of this itinerary we have presumed a stay of 2 days. Here follows a selection of Florence's attractions.

'Florence the Fair' (Firenze la Bella), the ancient capital of Tuscany, lies between the hills of the Arno valley in northern Tuscany.

The Etruscans were the first to inhabit this area, they settled on the hills at Fiesole. There was a Roman city called Florentia near the site of the Ponte Vecchio, however, the Romans had little, if anything, to do with Florence's rise to power at the beginning of the 13th century. This can be mainly attributed to the fortunes of war and trade.

During the Middle Ages Florence was first allied to the Guelphs, however, the Ghibellines defeated the Guelphs at Montaperti. Then the Guelphs fought back and in 1266 they finally won the city and established government by the 'Signoria', thus making Florence the mistress of all Tuscany bar Siena and Lucca.

In 1434 the Medici family came to power and laid the foundation for Florence's ultimate glory, the Renaissance. After this, there followed a rather unstable period of government, alternating between republics and Medicis, nevertheless Florence eventually became part of the Grand Duchy in 1530. So, a new era began. The city was governed by the Medici Dukes and then the Hapsburg-Lorraines. It grew more and more powerful. In 1555 Siena surrendered, and in 1847 Lucca succumbed; resulting in Tuscany's entrance into the Kingdom of Italy in 1859.

Today, the city is very much lived in. Its exquisitely preserved and restored monuments are both worked-in and prayed-in by modern Florentines. Although bustling with commerce and noisy traffic, Florence is a sophisticated jewel, and possesses a congenial and romantic atmosphere oddly similar to that of traffic-free Venice.

Historically it is rich, and there is so much to look at, that one could not possibly expect you to appreciate it to the full in just a few days, therefore, we suggest, that from the selection of information which follows, you sift through and visit the places which most appeal to you during these two days.

Apart from the Renaissance grandeur, this city abounds with luxurious shops. Jewellers, antique shops, fashion houses, leather boutiques full of the world's greatest footwear and accessories, are at your disposal, whether you buy from them or just gaze into them.

Sit and peruse life from a café in the Piazza della Repubblica, and feed the pigeons in the Cathedral Square. Stop for exotic ice-creams to cool yourself down in one of the numerous Gelateria as you wander, and seek out the lesser-known trattoria tucked away in the city's narrow, cobbled streets.

Through the centre of Florence flows the river Arno. It was on the banks of this river that Alighieri Dante (1265-1321) made his contribution to the Italian language. The purest Italian is spoken in this region even today. Either side of this river, which has broken its banks fifty times in Florence's history, are embankments that were built during the 19th century to protect against flood.

On the 4th of November 1966, Florence experienced the worst flood disaster ever recorded. In certain areas of the city the water rose to a staggering 23 feet. Mud and oil gushed everywhere, causing damage to literally hundreds of precious paintings, sculptures and frescoes, and more than a million priceless manuscripts. Florentines returned to their city from all over Italy, even before the waters had receded, to embark on the long and painful task of restoration. With the aid of donations from art lovers all over the world, the city of the Renaissance has now been restored to its former glory, and waits to greet you once again.

Piazza del Duomo

The religious centre of Florence is the Piazza del Duomo or Cathedral Square. The Cathedral of Saint Mary of the Flowers (Santa Maria del Fiore) is both impressive in its grand appearance, and its massive size. It can hold more than

20,000 people at one time. The cathedral takes the form of a Latin cross, it has three naves, and is the third longest church in the world. The first being St Peter's in Rome, and the second St Paul's in London. The cathedral stands on the site of the ancient church of St Reparata (one of the city's first patron saints), a small part has been excavated and can be visited from inside.

This magnificent building was initiated in 1296 by Arnolfo di Cambio, for a larger cathedral than ever before was deemed necessary to glorify Florence's newly found status. He died in 1302 and how much work had been completed by this time is unknown. In 1331 the Arte della Lana (Wool Guild), took over the project and appointed Giotto as 'Capomaestro'. First he started to construct the Campanile. This elegant slim square tower was almost completed by his pupil Andrea Pisano. The panoramic terrace was conceived by Talenti and finished in 1359.

As far as we know it was not until 1355 with Francesco Talenti that work recommenced on the cathedral itself. Based on Cambio's original plans, but with other architects, the majority of the cathedral, save the dome and facade, was completed by about 1417.

The dome, which is the cathedral's crowning glory, and holds sway over the entire city, can be seen from all the surrounding hills. It proved a major technical problem to construct. Due to the brilliance of the joint design of Brunelleschi and Ghiberti this architecturally historic dome, which is 348 ft tall, was begun in 1418. It took, not surprisingly, fourteen years to build, but was erected without the aid of a supporting frame. In 1436 Pope Eugenius IV consecrated the cathedral.

The facade, which is decorated with a series of statues and marble mosaics, was added during the last century. The white marble is from Carrara; the green from Prato; and the red from the Maremma in southern Tuscany.

Internally, our first impression was that of disappointment, for the Gothic interior seems cold and nude.

It does of course, contain many fascinating items. A bronze shrine by Lorenzo Ghiberti holds the remains of Florence's first Bishop, St Zenobius, and there is a glorious round stained-glass window by the same artist.

The most interesting work housed here is that of Vasari and Federico Zuccari.

It is an enormous fresco of the Last Judgement on the interior of Brunelleschi's dome.

In front of the Cathedral stands the octagonal, Romanesque baptistry of St John, which was constructed during the 11th and 12th centuries, on the site of a former Roman temple of Mars. The internal surface of this dome is covered with fantastic Byzantine style mosaics showing scenes from the Creation, the Life of St John and the Last Judgement, dominated by an enormous picture (25 ft high approx.) of Christ the King. To the right of the apse is the tomb of Antipope John XXIII, who was a friend of Cosimo the elder. This remarkable work is by Donatello and his assistant Michelozzo (1427). It is in fact one of the earliest tombs in the city. However, it is to the three sets of bronze gilded doors that the baptistry owes its international fame. The south door depicts scenes from the life of St John the Baptist and the eight virtues. It was carved by Andrea Pisano in 1330. The north door, by Ghiberti, shows the Life of Christ, however, the best known is the east door by the same artist. The door tells stories from the Old Testament. It was named 'The Door of Paradise' by Michelangelo, and who are we to dispute his verdict?

The Straw Market

The main attraction on the Mercato Nuovo (the Straw Market), built between 1547 and 1551, are the stalls selling leather, straw and lace goods, and the 17th-century bronze statue of a Boar. This is in fact a copy by Pietro Tacca of an original antique statue in the Uffizi. This splendid animal, known to the Florentines as 'Il Porcellino', the Piglet, is on the far side of the Loggia. Tradition has it that, if you stroke his nose, place a coin in his mouth, and the coin drops into the grate beneath, you will be sure to return to Florence.

The Ponte Vecchio

The original bridge, built around 996 AD, was situated a little upstream, on the site of an old Roman crossing. It was the only bridge across the river Arno until 1218.

The present Ponte Vecchio, the only bridge which was spared the devastation of the Second World War, dates back to 1345, this makes it one of the oldest bridges in the world. Up until the end of the 16th century, when the Grand

Duke Ferdinand I decreed that henceforth only goldsmiths should occupy the shops on this bridge, it was the domain of the butchers. A convenient situation — the Arno was used for waste disposal! No wonder the Grand Duke passed the decree. This regulation is still observed today and a bust of Benvenuto Cellini was erected in the centre of the bridge to honour the goldsmiths' heritage.

Above the shops, if you can take your eyes off the gems, is a covered passageway built by Vasari. The Vasarian Corridor was constructed in order that the Grand Duke Cosimo dei Medici could walk from the Pitti Palace to the Uffizi without getting wet.

The Santa Croce

Situated close to the river in the south-eastern quarter of the old town, the area which was the centre of the wool industry in medieval times, is the Gothic church of the Holy Cross.

It stands in the vast attractive open Piazza where Giuliano dei Medici once staged lavish jousts and starving Florentines used to attend football games during the 1530 siege of their city. The church which was designed first and foremost for the purposes of preaching, perhaps in the style of Arnolfo di Cambio, was begun in 1294/5 for the Franciscans, and not finished until 1442. Actually the facade and bell-tower were even later additions of 1857-63. If you look at the walls, you will clearly see the 16 ft high mark left by the Arno waters in the calamitous floods of '66.

The interior of the Santa Croce consists of a simple spacious nave and a slender apse adorned with 15th-century stained glass windows. Mention must be made of the organ which is reputed to be the largest in Italy. To the right of the altar is a chapel covered with frescoes depicting the life of St Francis. These were painted by Giotto and his pupils in about 1320 but have, of course, deteriorated since the flood. The chancel walls are clothed with frescoes by Agnolo Gaddi (1380) of the legend of the Holy Cross.

At the far end of the north transept is a crucifix by Donatello. The wonderfully carved pulpit with scenes from the life of St Francis, was sculpted by Benedetto da Maiano between 1472 and 1476.

Most interesting of all among this Church's treasures are perhaps the tombs, which contain many illustrious Italians. Among them are:– Michelangelo, whose body was smuggled out of Rome in a wooden box, and who was given the greatest funeral in Florentine history; Rossini (1792-1868), *The Barber of Seville*; Galileo (1564-1642); and Dante. Dante's tomb to the dismay of the Florentines contains no body, because his real grave is in Ravenna where he died.

The Pazzi Chapel is adjacent to the cloisters of the Santa Croce and was Brunelleschi's last creation, unfortunately left incomplete.

The Uffizi

The architect responsible for this palace, which was commissioned on the order of Cosimo I to extend and connect the city's offices of administration, was again Vasari. The palace took 14 years to complete. In the niches of the pillars along the portico have been placed 19th-century sculptures of important Tuscans, such as St Antonino, by Giovanni Dupré (1854) and Niccolo Machiavelli by Lorenzo Bartolini (1846).

The Uffizi, is a good example of an historical building with a present day working function. The State archives are located in the lower floors, and contain a library of documentation of the history of Florence and Tuscany, and on the third floor the Uffizi houses one of the largest art collections in the world; the walls are hung with the works of Florentine, Venetian, Dutch and German masters.

The numerous rooms can take many hours to view, so it would be quite impossible to describe all their priceless contents here.

Works include:

An Annunciation   — by Leonardo da Vinci
An Annunciation   — by Simone Martini
The Birth of Venus   — by Botticelli
The Holy Family   — by Michelangelo
The Virgin Mary   — by Raphael
Two paintings of Venus — by Titian
and two outstanding examples of the Danube school by A. Altodorfer.

The Palazzo Vecchio

Sometimes referred to as the Palazzo della Signoria, i.e. the Council chamber, this palace is still today the heart of Florence's civic centre. It is an imposing gothic-style building complete with battlements and parapet walks, and crowned by a 308 ft high tower which helps to soften its rather severe facade. It was built in the late 13th century to replace the original Bargello and finished some 120 years before the cathedral.

The palace is open to the public, and behind its facade you will discover a contrasting elegant interior. The courtyard is bright and in its centre is a copy of the delightful statue of Putto (Cherub) by Verrochio (the original is inside). Visit the halls of the five hundred frescoes, by Vasari and his school. This throne-room was embellished with these giant frescoes of Florentine victories by Cosimo I. Michelangelo's statue 'Victory', is also housed here. It is interesting to think that three hundred years later the first Italian National Government sat here.

Don't miss the Studiolo Hall, another gem designed by Vasari.

The second floor consists of the lavishly decorated apartments of Eleonora of Toledo (Cosimo I's wife). Nearby is the Hall of the Lilies (Sala dei Gigli), full of blues, golds, and bright frescoes by Ghirlandaio. Then go on to the Guardaroba. This room is lined with panelled cupboards painted with 16th-century maps. The great treasures of the Medici family were once stored here. In the adjoining room is Verrochio's original winged goblin.

This is, of course, only a brief resume of the palace. Spend some time here if possible and climb up to the top of the tower and treat yourself to the most sensational panorama in Florence.

Galleria dell'Accademia

The Academy was originally an art school founded by Cosimo I. In the 18th century an exhibition hall was added to further aid the students in their studies. A large collection from several schools was set up under the supervision of the Grand Duke Petro Leopoldo I in 1784. The building houses a vast number of 13th- to 16th-century Italian paintings including works by Cassone Adimari, Taddeo Gaddi and Giovanni da Milano. Its fame though is due to the seven works of Michelangelo in the gallery, the most renowned of which is the celebrated 'David', which was sculpted between 1501 and 1505 when the artist was only 25 years old. The statue was brought here from the Piazza della Signoria in 1873 to protect it from the elements.

On the right of 'David' is a bronze bust of Michelangelo himself, by his close friend and pupil Daniele da Volterra. The Academy (Via Ricasoli 60) is open mornings only and closed Mondays.

Piazza Michelangelo

From the Piazza Michelangelo there are the most spectacular views of the city below, and in the distance the hills of Fiesole. It was from these hills that Leonardo da Vinci first experimented with flight. In the centre of the square is a reproduction of Michelangelo's 'David' and the four allegorical statues found on the Medicean tombs in San Lorenzo.

Just above this Piazza stands yet another great piece of Florentine Romanesque architecture, the church of San Miniato al Monte. Erected between the 11th and 13th centuries, this church has a gracious white and green marble facade which glistens in the late afternoon sun. Perhaps this is why this church is a favourite for weddings. St Miniato was an early Christian who was martyred in the 3rd century. It is said that he carried his severed head up to here from the city and placed it on the ground of the present day church. The interior is endowed with inlaid marble, has a fine chapel and the tomb of the Cardinal of Portugal who died in Florence.

Note: Since the square is a major tourist attraction, refreshments here are hardly the best value for money.

Restaurants in Florence are so numerous that it is hardly necessary to point you in the right direction here. They range from first class, glamorous, expensive establishments to small cafés of every nationality for Florence, like London and Paris, is a cosmopolitan city. In the Piazza della Republica we tried several ristorante/trattoria where one can sit under a parasol and watch Florentine life whilst sipping Chianti and sampling some of the best dishes in Italy.

The Fertile Plains

DAY 9

From Florence to Arezzo

Today you must leave Florence and take the short drive to Arezzo, a town which still preserves her ancient history and whose sons gave so much to Italian art.

Travel Information
Total Mileage: approx. 46 miles, 2 hours including a stop for coffee

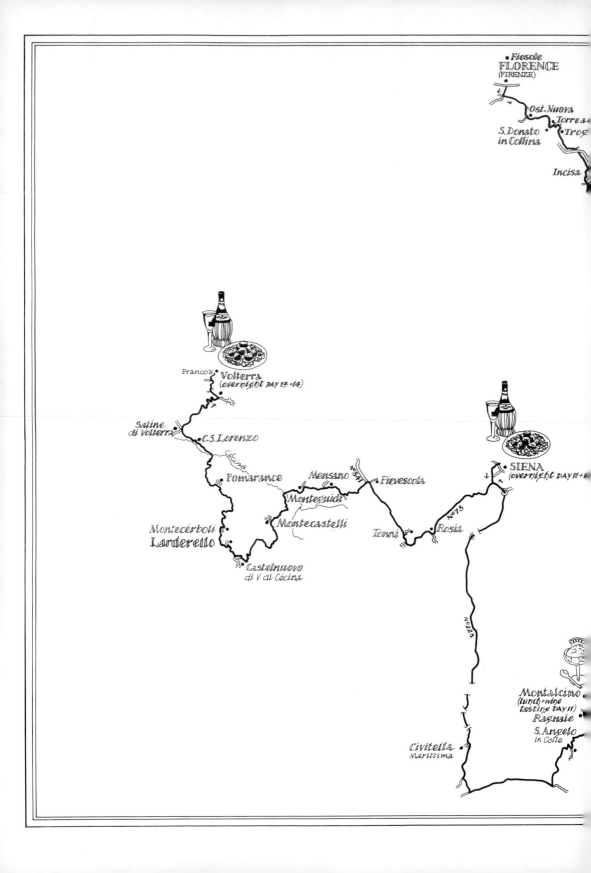

• Fiesole
FLORENCE
(FIRENZE)

Ost. Nuova
Torre a
S. Donato   Trog
in Collina   Trog

Incisa

Franco's • Volterra
(overnight DAY 13 +14)

Saline
di Volterra
• C.S. Lorenzo

Cécina
• Pomarance   • Mensano
                                    N°541
                     • Montequidi   • Pievescola

Montecérboli   • Montecastelli
Larderello   Tonni •   • Rosía
                                                    N°73
        • Castelnuovo
          di V di Cécina

                                    N°2325

                                        Montalcino
                                        (lunch + wine
                                        tasting DAY 11)
                                        Ragnaie
                                        S. Angelo
                                        in Colle
        Civitella •
        Marittima

SIENA
(overnight DAY 11 +1

N

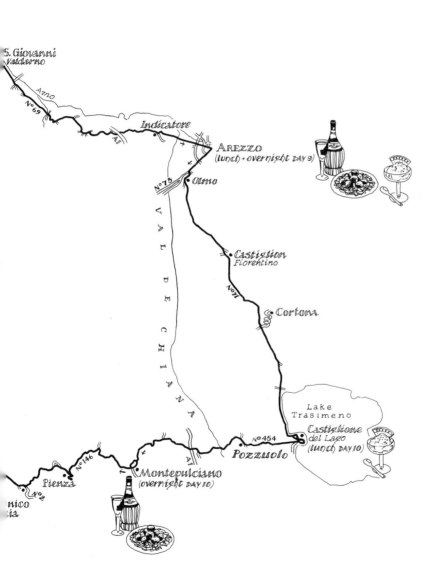

S. Giovanni
Valdarno

Arno

Nº 69

Indicatore

Arezzo
(lunch + overnight DAY 9)

Nº 73 • Olmo

V A L   D E   C H I A N A

• Castiglion
Fiorentino

Nº 71

• Cortona.

Lake
Trasimeno

Castiglione
del Lago
(lunch DAY 10)

Nº 454

Pozzuolo

A1

Nº 146

Montepulciano
(overnight DAY 10)

Pienza

Nº 2

nico
ia

Travels in Tuscany

Breakfast in Florence.

Leave Florence by the southern route taking the road No 222 towards Greve and then turn left towards the No 69 for Arezzo.

Stop for a good cheap coffee in San Donato in Collina, at the local bar.

The road between Florence and Arezzo runs through a varied landscape. At first the hillsides are abundant with olive trees, but at Troghi, the olives disappear giving way to grapes, maize, sunflowers and wheat. Small quiet villages nestle in fertile farmlands.

The road continues along the widening Arno valley, through an industrial zone characterized by gravel pits and areas of intense market gardening, until it winds back up through pleasant hills on its way to the old historically interesting town of Arezzo. Follow the signs to Arezzo Centro, and check in at your hotel.

Enjoy lunch at Arezzo before touring the town on foot.

The ancient town of Arezzo which lies in eastern Tuscany commands the fertile valleys of the Chiana, Tiber and Arno and thus is surrounded by a basin where cereals, fruit trees and vines flourish.

It is a city of Etruscan origin, which developed into a Roman stronghold guarding the Appennine passes and the road to Rome. Thus it has since early times been an important economic centre. In Roman times it was made famous by craftsmen who produced red glazed vases 'Corallini', which spread all over the Empire; today, apart from being rich in architectural monuments, Arezzo is world renowned for its antique market.

After a period of ecclesiastical rule, the town became independent. The ruling party was the Ghibellines. However, it was not long until they were defeated by the Guelphs (the rulers of Florence) at the battle of Campaldino near Poppi in 1289, and after a long fight the city finally surrendered to Florence in 1384. Soon after it was incorporated into the Medici Grand Duchy. The lower, new city is staggeringly modern, in contrast to the old city which still echoes the past.

The Cathedral

The Duomo San Donato, is situated at the highest point of the hill, in the Via Ricasoli, on the site of an earlier Benedictine church. It was begun in 1277, added to in 1313 and 1510, and actually not finally completed until the beginning of this century, when the facade was added.

The cathedral contains some notable works of art. In the north aisle can be seen a fresco of Mary Magdalen by Piero della Francesca. At the high altar is the 14th-century tomb of the cathedral's patron St Donatus, who was Bishop of Arezzo. But, perhaps the most outstanding works of art here are the stained glass windows, in the right-hand aisle, by Guillaume de Marcillat (1477-1529).

These four very striking windows show — *The Calling of Matthew*, *The Woman Taken in Adultery*, *The Cleansing of the Temple*, and *The Raising of Lazarus*.

Guillaume de Marcillat was born in La Châtre in France, apprenticed at Bourges, and later worked in Nevers where he decided to become a monk. However, his talent was widely recognised and he was summoned to work at the Vatican with Raphael and Michelangelo by Pope Julius II. In later life he settled in Arezzo. He was praised by Vasari for his skill in perspective and anatomy, especially in his windows in Arezzo's Duomo.

The Piazza Grande

A charming square, irregular in shape and bordered by palaces and houses of different periods, and therefore of varying architecture, which blend together perfectly.

The Pallazzo delle Logge, Palace of the Loggias, was built by Vasari in 1500. The Palazzo della Fraternita, Palace of Confraternity of the Laity, shows a combination of styles. The arch over the central door is Gothic as is the lower part of the entire building. The upper part is in what is called Pure Renaissance style. The central bas-relief, *Our Lady of Mercy*, and the statues in the niches either side of St Donato and St Gregory, are all by Bernado Gambarelli. The amazing clock tower was constructed according to a design by Vasari. The clock, a work by Felice da Fossato, is unique — it illustrates the theory of the renowned Egyptian astronomer, Ptolemy.

The Chiesa Santa Maria della Pieve, the parish church of St Mary, backs onto the Piazza Grande. Built during the 12th and 13th centuries, it is probably the largest and best illustration of Romanesque/Pisan architecture in the Arezzo region. Indeed it is considered by some to be the finest example in the whole of Tuscany.

The unusual tower, 'The Tower of a Hundred Holes', named after its forty double-arched windows, stretches sedately up into the skyline. A truly impressive landmark.

Compared with its sumptuously carved exterior, the interior of this church is rather severe, although extremely spacious, but it is worth noting the polyptych at the high altar by Pietro Lorenzetti (c. 1320).

In the centre of the old town is the church of San Francesco.

This plain-looking church in Franciscan Gothic style was begun in 1290 and has undergone extension and renovation right up to the present day. Its principal attractions are the celebrated frescoes by Piero della Francesca which recount the sixteen-part legend of the Holy Cross. Piero della Francesca (1410/20-92), was born close by in San Sepolcro.

The house where the poet and scholar Francesco Petrach (1304-74) was born in Via dell'Orto, was unfortunately destroyed. However, a new building was erected on the same site in the 16th or 17th century, which is now the headquarters of the Accadémia Petrarca di Léttere, Arti e Scienze.

In the Via XX Septembre, you will find the house which the painter, historian and architect Giorgio Vasari acquired in 1540. Between 1540 and 1548 he decorated the inside with a series of beautiful frescoes. These are worth seeing if the house is open, but unfortunately it is more often than not closed.

On the first Sunday in September each year the Piazza Grande is transformed for Arezzo's Saracen's Tournament (La Giostra del Saracino).

This ceremony commences with what is best described in English as 'Flag Juggling'. Wearing costumes from the 14th century, standard bearers display their flag-juggling skills in a drama of acrobatic dexterity, portraying the theme of 'War and Peace'.

After this display comes the Saracen Joust, a contest which dates back to the 13th century. Horsemen representing the four ancient quarters of the town attack a dummy figure with lances. The horsemen of the city quarter with the most points win the competition.

The whole ritual takes place to the beating of drums and trumpet fanfares.

We suggest that you dine at:
Ristorante Logge Vasari
Piazza Grande
Arezzo
Tel: (0575) 25894

As its name suggests this restaurant is set under the arches of the old Palazzo della Logge. Here you may dine by candlelight overlooking the attractive square.

We found the Prosciutto Nostrale e Melone excellent here.

Your hotel could reserve you a table, or call in during your promenade to ensure a loggia table.

Hotel Europa
Via Spinello 45
52100 Arezzo
Tel: (0575) 357701

A modern hotel in the new town, comfortable and very adequate for your overnight stay at Arezzo

Facilities:	Some rooms have air-conditioning
	Bar, telephone and TV
	All rooms have private bath or shower
Restaurant:	No
Rating:	★★★

USEFUL INFORMATION — AREZZO

Tourist Office:	E.P.T. Via della Madonna de Prato
Altitude:	296 metres (971 ft)
Population:	92,000
Main train station	

DAY 10

From Arezzo to Montepulciano

The drive from Arezzo to Montepulciano will take you across the wide alluvial plains of the Val di Chiana. Watch out for tobacco harvesting on your way. Lunch should be taken overlooking the peaceful water of Lake Trasimeno, and you will spend the night in Montepulciano, the home of Italy's rich 'Vino Nobile' wine.

Travel Information
Total Mileage — approx. 48 miles
Arezzo to Castiglione del Lago — approx. 30 miles, about 1 hour
Castiglione del Lago to Montepulciano — 18 miles, about 1 hour

After breakfast, leave Arezzo.

Opposite Arezzo station turn left and follow the sign Tutte le Direzione (all directions), and then the sign to Cortona/Perugia/Siena. After 3½ miles turn left onto the Perugia road the No 71. This road follows the Val di Chiana all the way to Lake Trasimeno. To your left you will see villages on the hillside, and on your right the wide green alluvial plains of the valley which is famous for the best beef cattle in Italy.

After about 30 miles you will arrive at Castiglione del Lago on the edge of the lake.

The garden of Tuscany, the Val di Chiana is the most extensive valley in the Appennine chain, it stretches over 500 square kilometres of organised farmland. Even as early as the 3rd century BC this valley must have been considered the granary of Etruria, since Hannibal, even after ransacking the area, was able to feed his entire army here, before defeating the Roman legions at the Battle of Trasimeno on the 24th June, 217 BC.

There is, in fact, archeological evidence to support the theory that the valley was cultivated by an early civilization. Underground tombs discovered at Camacia and Sodo prove that the Etruscans drained and cultivated this swamp. Sometime after the Romans, the valley, because it was no longer tended with the care and attention it needed, reverted to marshland once again. It was not until the Aretine engineer, Vittoria Fossombroni planned and carried out a reclamation of this land at the beginning of the 19th century, that the Val di Chiana was restored to its former productive capacity.

Castiglione del Lago

This little village is situated on a chalky promontory overlooking the largest lake in Central Italy — Lago Trasimeno. The silvery, misty waters of this fresh water lake cover approximately 50 square miles and have a circumference of 28 miles. Its northern banks are clothed with umbrella pines, cypresses, vineyards and olive groves, and along its shore fishermen sit mending their nets. In August the lake turns into a holiday resort frequented by the Italians, so it is best to avoid this month if you intend to do more than just visit for lunch. Innes and I decided on this location for lunch, even though it is just on the borders of Umbria, since the Hotel/Ristorante Miralago, offers samples of all sorts of fresh-water fish. A welcome change.

From the main road take the No 454 signposted to Montepulciano. This road passes through the little village of Pozzuolo, over undulating slopes and then down to the plain. Turn right, over the Autostrada and continue on, following the signs to Montepulciano. (*Note:* Not Monte. Staz.) As the landscape changes to become full of vines you will be able to see the town perched high up on the hill like an eagle's eyrie.

Montepulciano

Drive up the very steep narrow streets through the town to find a suitable place to park. Montepulciano like many of Tuscany's walled citadels has a one-way system, which can be somewhat confusing. The tourist office will supply you with a detailed map.

Check in to the hotel of your choice, and then take a leisurely walk around the historic streets.

View the 16th- to 17th-century Cathedral with its unfinished facade, shorn of the customary marble facing. Note how similar the Town Hall is to the Palazzo Vecchio in Florence, and indulge in some serious wine tasting.

According to ancient legend, the town was founded by an Etruscan King, but we do not know this for sure, because the town's history is not well documented until the 8th century AD. During the 8th, 9th and 10th centuries Montepulciano was an independent self-governing commune. From the 12th to 15th centuries, due to its strategic position and agricultural wealth, Montepulciano became involved in the long lasting wars between Florence and Siena. First allied to Florence, then Perugia in Umbria, the town eventually fell into Sienese hands. These three centuries of warfare also caused unrest and rivalry between the town's nobles, who fought among themselves for over 50 years to control their commune. This period witnessed the birth of some great men. The writer and poet, Angelo Ambrogini; Cardinal Cervini, who became Pope Marcellus II; and the theologian Roberto Cardinal Bellarmino, Galileo's rival.

In 1511 war ceased at last, and Montepulciano became part of Florentine territory, and when Cosimo dei Medici was elevated to Grand Duke of Tuscany in 1569, this town is said to have been his favourite.

Nowadays, the economic structure of this hilltop citadel is still based on agriculture and the flourishing vineyards, which produce the celebrated 'Vino Nobile'.

Thanks to its location, stretched along the thin crest of volcanic rock, Montepulciano, considered by some to be one of Tuscany's best preserved Renaissance towns, still remains as it was in its 16th and 17th century heyday.

We know, from a parchment dated 790 AD referring to the sale of a vineyard, that wine has been produced here since the 8th century, and from another document that Montepulciano's red wine was exported as early as 1350.

It was soon after this wine was described as 'The perfect wine for a nobleman to drink', by S. Lancerio, the sommelier to Pope Paul III, that it became known as 'Vino Nobile'. In the 17th century, the poet and author, Francesco Redi, proclaimed Montepulciano to be the King of all wines and hence its fame spread all over Europe.

The Vino Nobile, then, has a long heritage. In 1966 it was among Italy's first wines to be granted the government's guarantee of origin, the D.O.C.; and in 1981 it was the very first wine to be awarded the honour of the D.O.C.G.

On August 29, 1372 was first run the 'Bravio', which was a horse race through the citadel. Today the race, whilst it follows the original route, is run with barrels. Eight barrels representing the town's ancient divisions, weighing each about 80 Kg, are pushed through the streets.

The race starts, at the ringing of the Town Hall bell, in Sant'Agnese. They race uphill to the steps of the Cathedral. Before the race there is a grand procession in traditional 14th-century costume.

In the evening drive out of the citadel in the direction of Pienza to the Ristorante La Grotta, which is situated near the Renaissance church of San Biagio. This is really the only restaurant that we can recommend here, but it is not cheap.

Hotel/Ristorante Miralago
Piazza Mazzini 5
06061 Castiglione del Lago

The entrance to the restaurant is through the hotel from the Piazza Mazzini. Sen. Enzo Vernarecci purchased the Miralago in 1987 and plans to refurbish the entire building before the summer of 1988. Fresh fish from the lake will be his speciality in the Terrace restaurant together with local wines such as Cantina Sociace Trasimeno.

Ristorante La Grotta
Location San Biagio
Montepulciano
Tel: (0578) 757607

The Meublé Il Riccio
Via Talosa 21
53045 Montepulciano
Siena
Tel: (0578) 757713

An unusual place to stay, the Meublé Il Riccio is situated in a narrow street off the Piazza Grande and is entered through the mosaic museum, which has an extremely pretty courtyard. Mount the stairs to arrive in this attractive recently converted establishment which provides all modern comforts. It is open all year, but has no restaurant.

Rating: ★★

La Terrazza
Via Pie'al Sasso 16
Via di Votaia nel Corso 84
53045 Montepulciano
Siena
Tel: (0578) 757440

La Terrazza is a charming hotel with fourteen rooms with ensuite bathrooms and three mini-apartments, right in the heart of the historical centre. It has a pretty terrace but again no restaurant.

Rating: ★★

Hotel Il Borghetto
Via Borgo Buio 7
53045 Montepulciano
Siena
Tel: (0578) 757535

This small family run hotel provides modern comforts within a traditional setting. Most double rooms have bathroom facilities. No restaurant.

Rating: ★★

Note: Advance booking is advised for all of these hotels.

USEFUL INFORMATION — MONTEPULCIANO	
Tourist Office:	Via Ricci 9, just off the Piazza Grande, very good
Altitude:	605 metres (1985 ft)
Population:	nearly 15,000
Festivals:	1st May — Traditional fair and street market
	Last Sunday of August — The Barrels Race
Monte.Terme:	Health Spa in San Albino just 2½ mls towards Chianciano. Waters rich in sulphur and bromine are renowned for their healing qualities.

Villages and Vineyards

DAY 11

A journey across to the city which is famous for the red soils which gave their name to the colour, Burnt Sienna.

Travel Information
Total Mileage: approx: 69 miles
Montepulciano to Montalcino — 23 miles, about 2 hours allowing for time in Pienza
Montalcino to Siena — approx. 46 miles, about 2 hours

Travels in Tuscany

Breakfast at Montepulciano.

In the morning, drive the short distance westwards on the No SS 146 to Pienza for coffee.

Pienza

This picturesque little town is known by the Tuscans as 'La Perla de Rinascimento', The Pearl of the Renaissance, and it is easy to see why.

Originally Pienza was an insignificant village called Corisgnano. However, Enea Silvio Piccolomini (1405-64) who became Pope Pius II in 1458, decided to transform Corisgnano into his Utopia. Consequently he commissioned the local architect Bernardo Gamberelli (also known as B. Rossellino) to design what became the first Tuscan town ever to be built to a regular plan.

Work began in 1459 and the mini-city, christened Pienza by its inhabitants in memory of Pope Pius, was completed three years later.

The Cathedral which is located in the main square is quite exquisite. Its neat geometric interior is refreshingly light.

The shops in this almost too perfect setting, are full of every type of delicacy available in Tuscany. Pienza is particularly noted for excellent cheeses, especially Pecorino.

Leaving Pienza, take the road No SS 146. Turn right at S. Quirico onto the Siena road (No 2) and then turn left off the main road to Montalcino.

Montalcino

Nestling in green rolling hills south of Siena, lies the quiet little unassuming town, called Montalcino. This town, however, has a reputation for producing a superb red wine, Brunello di Montalcino. What better reason could there be to visit it for a gourmet luncheon?

There are two equally excellent restaurants for you to choose from.

The first is **La Cucina di Edgardo** in Via S. Saloni 33, in the town itself. (Tel: 0577 848232.)

Both in Milan and at Montalcino, Edgardo offers an interesting and varied menu including wine tastings, for lunch and dinner. His imaginative menus are based on the season and inspiration.

Whatever dish you choose, it will always have been carefully thought out, prepared with fresh ingredients and accompanied by a suitably impressive wine.

Excellent cuisine at a reasonable price. Credit Cards — Amex.

The second is the **Ristorante Poggio Antico** (Tel: 0577 849200) which is located a few miles outside Montalcino on the Grosseto road.

Food, service and wine here are all exceedingly good; however the setting amongst the vines is magical. On a beautiful sunny day, out of the two, this would be our personal preference winning on situation alone. *Note:* Closed on Tuesdays. Credit Cards — Diners Club and Amex.

After lunch set off for Siena.

The road signed to Grosseto takes you over to the SS 223; it is bordered by acres and acres of neatly tended vineyards, interspersed with copses and olive groves, and offers the most magnificent views.

Cut across to the SS 223 and follow it all the way to Siena, turning off to the city centre at the exit 'Porta San Marco'. Look out for the paddy fields either side of the road on nearing Siena. They are an incredible sight.

Dinner and two nights accommodation in Siena.

In Siena we are pleased to recommend four hotels. The first two being right in the heart of the city, the third one just outside, and the last, a villa in the Sienese countryside. Contrary to the usual system, here we are happy to recommend the hotel restaurants.

Hotel/Pensione Palazzo Ravizza
Pian dei Mantellini 34
Siena
Tel: (0577) 280462
Telex: 575304

A converted 17th-century mansion just five minutes walk from the cathedral and the Piazza del Campo. The Palazzo has been in the family for about 200 years, and at one point was used as a school teaching music and Italian to young ladies from noble families. From the beautiful gardens there are views of the Tuscan hills. Bed and breakfast or half-board accommodation are both available. This hotel has the benefit of a first class restaurant.

Open all year round
Rooms: 30 all with private bathrooms
Rating: ★★★/★

The Hotel Santa Caterina
Via Enea Silvio Piccolomina 7
Siena
Tel: (0577) 221105

This late 18th-century building was transformed into an hotel in 1986. It has 19 rooms each with private bathroom, air conditioning and telephone. Large garden and veranda, where breakfast may be enjoyed.

Closed: Nov. 15th to 1st March
Food: Bed and breakfast only
Rating: ★★★

The Hotel Garden
Via Custoza 2
53100 Siena
Tel: (0577) 47056/44392

Affording a splendid panoramic view over the city, this comfortable hotel is situated away from the main bustle of the city in a 16th-century patrician house. Not quite as intimate as the other three being a much larger operation.

Facilities:	Large garden, swimming pool, telephones in all rooms, air conditioned bar, good restaurant, ample parking.
Rating:	★★★/★

The Hotel Villa Belvedere
53034 Colle Val d'Elso
Siena
Tel: (0577) 920966

Built in 1795, this villa was once the residence of Ferdinand III, Archduke of Austria and Grand Duke of Tuscany in 1820. Only 7½ miles from Siena it is a pleasant place to rest a while.

The hotel has bedrooms with bath and shower, internal telephones and central heating. The restaurant offers a 'rich' menu of typical Tuscan dishes. Try 'Pici' a type of pasta from nearby Monteriggioni.

Closed:	Nov. 15th to 1st March
Facilities:	Wonderful setting, large car park, car hire, bed and breakfast, half-board or full board
Rating:	★★★★

USEFUL INFORMATION — SIENA

Altitude:	322 metres (1056 ft)
Population:	64,000
Tourist Office:	Piazza Il Campo
Others:	Camping, Main-line station
Festivals:	The most famous is the 'Palio', July 2nd and August 16th (see p. 127).

USEFUL INFORMATION — MONTALCINO

Population:	Approx. 6000
Facilities:	Good wine, shops. No Tourist Office
Altitude:	567 metres

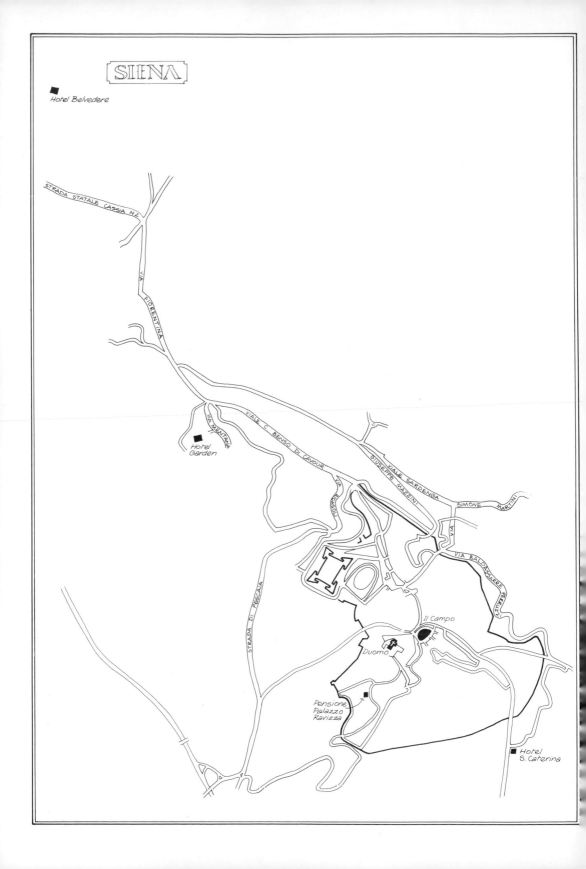

DAY 12

Step back into the past in Siena.

A city where medieval traditions are retained and where the new blends harmoniously with the old. Siena invites you to stroll along its Gothic streets lined with palaces and mansions.

The historic and artistic centre has been excellently conserved and traffic free, so there is no need to dodge mopeds, and since there is very little pollution the stone buildings are still their original lovely colour, 'Burnt Sienna'.

Travels in Tuscany

Breakfast in Siena.

Siena

The Sienese like to be thought of as the sons of Rome, and therefore they chose Romulus and Remus suckling the She-wolf as both their City symbol, and their balzana (coat of arms). This is coloured black and white — the colours of two legendary horses ridden by Aschelus and Senio, sons of Remus who are supposed to have ridden here from Rome and founded Siena.

Whether there is any truth in this legend is unlikely, although we do know for certain that Siena was Roman during the rule of Augustus, for he formed a colony and named the village Sena Julia.

In Medieval times, after Lombard and French domination the Bishops became rulers of the city (11th-century). In 1147 the Sienese overthrew Bishop Rainero and became a free community, ruled by its inhabitants. From then, until 1555, she constituted one of the two republics of Tuscany (the other one was Lucca) that maintained the longest period of autonomy before joining the supremacy of Florence.

During the period of independence the internal life of Siena was unstable. Full of continuous quarrels between families and factions, so much so that the religious figures of the city were always pleading for peace. Of the many governments of Siena, one to remember in particular was that of the Nine (1291-1355), which produced the internal stability and years of prosperity needed for a cultural growth.

Siena waged bloody wars with her neighbouring Tuscan and Umbrian cities, and above all with Florence.

The long struggle between the Sienese Ghibellines and the Florentine Guelphs gave rise to alternating victories. However, the war ended when the Florentines, with the aid of the Spanish army, forced Siena to surrender on the 17th April, 1555.

The National Gallery

The National Gallery (Pinacoteca Nazionale) is housed in the Palazzo Buonsignori, Via S. Pietro 29. Built around 1450, it is amongst the most refined examples of Gothic civil architecture in Siena. The Palace was turned into an Art Gallery in the second half of the 18th century. Now the home of the National Gallery, it is comprised of 700 paintings in 37 rooms. All the most important Sienese masters are represented here together with Flemish and German works. A chronological tour begins on the second floor.

The gallery is open mornings only (9am-2pm).

The Cathedral

The Duomo Santa Maria, at the highest point in the city of Siena is, in our opinion, the most impressive of all the cathedrals in Tuscany. It is not known when the first church was built on this site, but the present one was started in 1229. The dome was completed in 1264, prior to the heightening of the nave, and so it looks as though it is in effect set into the nave. The choir was extended eastward over the baptistry about 1317. At one time, there was a scheme to extend this church to make it the largest cathedral in Italy, however, this never came to pass since the foundations were found to be inadequate for such a colossal building and the population had been decimated by the Plague in 1348.

The facade is a fine example of Italian Gothic architecture, it is faced in white, green, and red marble and decorated with sculpted figures, most of which were renewed during the 19th century. Flanked by two pinnacles the triangular shaped pediment, and low gables either side, are composed of the most wonderful 19th-century mosaics by Venetian artists. The 'light' Campanile, by Neroccio (1484), is Romanesque. It was erected as a monument to Bishop Tommaso Piccolomini del Testa. Above the central door is a rose window depicting the Last Supper. Fragments of the incomplete extension can be seen at the end of the right-hand transept.

This cathedral boasts a unique floor. It comprises 56 panels depicting stories from the Old Testament, Sibyls, Biblical scenes and allegories, it took over 200 years, from about 1370 to complete. The more intricate panels are the most recent. Some of the panels have been restored, some replaced by copies, and some can only be seen at certain times, as they are covered up with wood to prevent further deterioration of these marble masterpieces.

Note also, the octagonal white marble pulpit by Niccolo Pisano and his pupils.

At the back of the cathedral is the baptistry, which was constructed at the same time as the extension of the choir, which it actually holds up. The fresco-covered vaulting, painted in 1450 by artists including Lorenzo di Pietro (1412-86) was badly restored in the late 19th century.

The font is both beautiful and elaborate. Its six sides are enhanced by gilded copper reliefs: *The Feast of Herod*, by Donatello, *The Life of St John*, by Ghiberti, *St John the Baptist Preaching*, by Giovanni di Turino, *Zacharia Driven from the Temple*, by Iacopo della Quercia, *The Birth of St John the Baptist*, by Turino di Sano, and *The Baptism of Christ*, by Ghiberti.

The Piazza del Campo

This scallop-shaped square, surrounded by gracious buildings and forming the junction of eleven streets, is situated right in the very centre of Siena. The most striking building here is the Palazzo Pubblico, the Town Hall. This graceful Gothic palace, was begun in 1297. The ground and first floors were completed by 1310, the central section and right wing by 1342 and the left wing in 1680.

The 290 ft high tower, the Torre del Mangia, was built between 1325 and 1344, and was named after the chief bell-ringer in the Middle Ages — he never stopped eating!

At the foot of the tower is found the Cappella di Piazza, which was erected in 1378 to commemorate the end of the tragic plague of 1348. To the right of this monument in a courtyard, the Cortile del Podesta, is a statue of Mangia, the famous glutton. Within, the Palazzo Pubblico is full of exceptional works of art. On the upper floors is the Museo Civico which contains the original carvings (by Iacopo della Quercia) from the Fonte Gaia (pool in the Piazza del Campo), and the entrance to the tower. If you can endure the strenuous climb up more than 300 steep narrow steps, you will be rewarded by a spectacular panorama of the city.

Twice a year, on July 2nd and August 16th the Piazza del Campo becomes the biggest tourist attraction in all Siena, when it is transformed into the setting for the colourful exciting pageant — the Palio.

While there is documentary evidence that animal races have been held here since the 13th century, the authentic Palio, which is still staged in its original form today, dates back to the 17th and 18th centuries. The race on the 2nd July, goes back to 1660 and is in honour of the Madonna of Provenzan (apparently she miraculously appeared to Provenzan Salvani, the hero of the battle of Montaperti). The second race on the 16th August started in 1702, and it is dedicated to the Madonna of the Assumption.

The Piazza is laid out for these two events well in advance. The central 'shell' is barricaded off and the external part is filled with wooden grandstands for the spectators and judges.

The ring-shaped area is left free as the race-track is covered with sand, and mattresses are placed in strategic positions to protect jockeys in their frequent falls.

From 17 horses (originally there were 59), only ten can run at once. They are chosen by the allocation of lots, a deal known as the 'Tratta'.

During the three days prior to the 'Palio', rehearsals are run to accustom the horses to the track, because this is an extremely dangerous race. If any horse should happen to die during rehearsal, its 'Contrada' (district) is eliminated, but it will, however, take its place in the parade, bearing the horse's hooves on a silver platter.

The whole of Siena is then dressed with flags and banners.

On the morning of the great day, Mass is held at 7 am in the chapel in the Piazza, and the standards of the Contradas are exhibited either in the church of St Mary of Provenzano (for July 2nd), or in the Cathedral (for August 16th).

In the afternoon each Contrada's horse is blessed in the Parish church. By this time enormous crowds are gathering in the square.

The Grand Procession and the race take place in the evening between 5pm

127

and 7pm. The majority of this time is taken up with processions, marches and flag juggling, and finally the Triumphal cart. Drawn by four oxen, this elaborate coach carried the city flag and banner, the prize of the race, around the square. The Palium (the prize) is a silk banner depicting the Virgin Mary; it is then delivered to the Judge by pages.

Now is the time for the jockeys and horses to prepare themselves for their moment of glory. Whip in hand, which is used not only to encourage their horse but to unsaddle their rivals, they line up, in the order in which they have been drawn, at the starting point. To win, they must complete three laps around the track. For your information, this is the only horse race that I know of in which a riderless horse is allowed to win. After the race, the winning jockey is carried into the square shoulder high. Thereafter follows a service of thanksgiving, in the appropriate church, which is attended by all the jockey's supporters and friends.

The Journey Ends

DAY 13

Siena to Volterra

Today's excursion takes you through an untamed landscape rich with hunting grounds, past a unique power station, and then on to your final destination Volterra. Volterra stands alone dominating an area which can only be described as Italy's Holy Land.

Travel Information
Total Mileage: 70 miles, about 2-2½ hours.

Breakfast in Siena.

Leave Siena and return to the SS 2 (Superstrada) northbound. Exit at Porta S. Marco onto the SS 73 signposted to Massa Maritima and Roccastrade.

The road to Rosia is bordered by fields of maize. The road then follows the right bank of a small river through a lush forested steep-sided valley. After sixteen miles, turn right onto the road to Colle di Val d'Elsa, No 541.

Here the landscape is more open, the soils are red and the woodlands stocked with game for the hunting season.

After a further 7 miles turn left to Radicondoli and Mensano, and soon after (about 3½ miles) turn right, signed to Monteguidi, and then 2 miles further on, left to Monteguidi and Larderello.

Drive up into the typically Tuscan tiny village of Monteguidi for coffee, in its only café, the Indios. The signora will make you most welcome. Return to the road and turn right. Cross over the river Cecina and follow the winding road through a forest of chestnut trees and oaks. In the Autumn this is a favourite place for truffle and mushroom hunting.

Just before Montecastelli, a village perched high up on the rocks, turn left to Castelnuovo. (*Note:* do not follow the Larderello sign here.) All of a sudden a most contrasting sight will appear before you. To your left you will see the Medieval village of Castelnuovo, cut into the hillside; and in front to the right, your first glimpse of the shimmering pipes and smoking cooling towers of an extraordinary geothermal power station.

Drive on to Larderello.

Larderello

Larderello sits amidst the metal-bearing Tuscan hills on Montecerboli. A former mining village, it is now a monstrous man-made eyesore, which scars the land with a 'spaghetti junction' of long pipelines.

None the less it is an interesting feat of engineering. From the volcanic ground beneath, emerge jets of steam ($212°-280°$F), and chemical substances. Boric acid and other materials are recovered from underground reservoirs, and the steam is harnessed to produce power for electricity.

On reaching the medieval town of Pomarance, a definite change in vegetation occurs. You enter into the barren dry land of Volterra. In Saline di Volterra where, as its name suggests, there are several salt mines, turn right to Volterra, which is reached by a very long series of steep bends.

Drive to your hotel, and then go into the city for lunch.

Volterra

An afternoon stroll to Le Balze (the cliffs).

These inhospitable cliffs are on the northwest edge of Volterra. The cliffs, which once housed the oldest Etruscan burial ground in Tuscany, were formed by the incessant erosion of layers and layers of ancient rock.

In 1140 they swallowed up an 8th-century Lombard church dedicated to St Giusto and the convent of St Marco. A new church was built, but this was also engulfed between 1617 and 1627.

The old Abbey, however, still remains, although it has been closed since the monks were forced to abandon it in the 1860s after it suffered severe damage by an earthquake. There are plans to restore the Abbey and some work has already commenced.

Look over the traces of the Etruscan city walls at an unforgettable scene. The view from here is breathtaking indeed, especially at sunset. Be careful here, since even today the Volterraneans believe that he who defies the danger of these cliffs will never return. This century only two people have escaped with their lives after accidents here.

Dinner and overnight at Volterra.

Travels in Tuscany

The Albergo Villa Nencini
Borgo S. Stefano
56048 Volterra
Tel: (0588) 86386

A charming villa-style hotel with an enchanting garden and ample car parking, situated towards Le Balze. Our first choice even though it has no restaurant.

Rating: ★★

Hotel San Lino
Via San Lino 26
56048 Volterra
Tel: (0588) 85250

This hotel is found in the historical centre of the city. The building was originally an old convent, today it offers good modern comforts and a warm atmosphere.

Rooms:	43, all with bathrooms
Facilities:	Dining room (although the food here is strictly hotel style) lifts, TV, bar and garden garage (extra charge)
Credit Cards:	all
Rating:	★★★

Il Pozzo
Via delle Prigioni
Volterra

A wonderful little restaurant frequented by the local Italians. This normally means that the food is good, and it certainly is here. Mario will look after you, advise you on what to choose, and since his portions are not over large, you will be able to wade pleasurably through the entire menu. Ask Mario if you can try his delicious lemon and peach home-made liqueur.

Credit Cards:	Amex and Visa

Il Poggio
Via Matteotti 39
Volterra
Tel: (0588) 85257

This is a new restaurant which specialises in Tuscan and Volterranean dishes, including game.

Ristorante a biscondola
di Nicola Dipaolantonio
56048 Volterra
Tel: (0588) 85197

Just below the city on the road to Cecina and Livorno is another delightful restaurant with a terrace.

When we ate there, we asked the proprietor to bring us a selection of Chef's specialities. We started with a selection of Crostini, then a plate of local charcuterie — Duck salami, Smoked venison, Smoked kid and wild boar sausage. Next came pancakes filled with soft cheese. A mixed salad. Pasta and risotto. Charcoal-grilled wild-boar chops, rabbit cooked with olives and finally baby venison steak.

Not surprisingly we were too full to try a pudding, but we did enjoy every part of the meat. We washed it all down with local red wine and a bottle of Italian Champagne, and were amazed at the reasonable bill. Watch out — no credit cards, so go armed with cash.

USEFUL INFORMATION — VOLTERRA

Altitude:	531 metres (1742 ft)
Population:	15,000
Others:	Good campsite with swimming pool
Speciality:	Alabaster goods
Festivals:	Regular musical concerts in the Piazza Priori (Summer). 1st Sunday in September 'Astiludio', similar to the Joust in Arezzo.

The Monastery, Volterra

DAY 14

A day in Volterra

Discover this peaceful hilltop city on foot, before embarking on your homeward journey.

We do hope you have enjoyed your holiday and will return home, both rested and exhilarated.

Travels in Tuscany

Breakfast in Volterra.

Volterra

The first settlers here were the Villanovans. We know this from archeologists, who discovered clay vases containing human ashes, and funeral apparel, which they were able to date as 9th century BC. Discoveries from the 7th century BC provide us with evidence of burial rituals, proving the start of a new Etruscan civilization here around this time. The Etruscans named their city 'Velathri'.

The archeological remains, now housed in the Museo Etrusco, help us to understand and reconstruct in part the development of Velathri.

A small, yet powerful state, Volterra was governed by Lucamore, and a council of nobles. The lower classes engaged themselves in commercial activities. The flourishing city developed quickly, it grew to cover an area of 116 hectares, stretching as far south as the Maremma and right over to the Val di Chiana, by the 4th century BC. To protect themselves against invasion the Etruscans enclosed their state with an immensely long wall, 23620 ft long, and in some parts 36 ft tall.

These people lived in houses composed of three rooms and an internal courtyard. Outside the city walls they built vast, decorated necropoli for their dead, for they believed that the spirit lived on after death and must be well cared for. The dead person was therefore interred with his or her worldly possessions.

Little is known of life here until the date, verified as 298 BC, when Volterra was defeated by Lucio Scipione Barbato and was obliged to ally with Rome. During this time (the second Punic War) the State of Volterra supplied Rome with materials and other equipment for shipbuilding.

Volterra came under the rule of Florence in 1361, and was later incorporated into the Grand Duchy of Tuscany.

Today, Volterra relies chiefly on tourism for its economy together with its thriving alabaster industry.

Just a few miles down the road towards Pontederra, on the right is a very sharp turning into an unmade road (see map). Follow this road past several farms and houses to its destination.

This farmhouse is owned by the Marzetti family, and it is here that Franco, a true craftsman, produces traditional and modern articles in alabaster.

He will be pleased to demonstrate his craft to you, as he did for us.

Monticatini Alto

Recipes

A Sample Dinner Party Menu*

MENU

Antipasti
Antipasto misto, Crostini and Funghi Marinati
wine — Vernaccia di San Gimignano

. . .

Zuppa
Zuppa Volterrana
(served in small ramekins)

. . .

Secondi Piatti
Saltimbocca alla Romana
wine — Vino Nobile di Montepulciano

. . .

Dolci
Zabaione
wine — Vin Santo

* All recipes in the following section are for 4 persons unless otherwise stated

Antipasti

Antipasto misto con fichi o melone

A selection of salami and prosciutto ham served with either fresh figs or ripe melon.

It is important to slice the meats as thinly as possible and make sure that the fruit is beautifully ripe.

Allow 3 figs or a quarter of a small melon per person.

Crostini

These are pieces of lightly fried bread spread with different toppings served either hot or cold. Three recipes for the toppings follow, so why not serve all three to make an unusual, colourful starter which is typically Tuscan. Allow one piece of bread per person, instead of 2, if serving this way. Make up the croutons and sauces separately, and re-heat under the grill just before serving.

Alla Fiorentina
Chicken livers on fried croutons

8 oz chicken livers, finely chopped
1 small onion, finely chopped
2 anchovy fillets, chopped
1 dessert spoon of caster sugar
¼ pt Italian white dry wine
Black pepper and mixed herbs to taste

Fry the chicken livers, onion and anchovy in a little butter or olive oil until cooked (about 10 mins.). Then add the wine, sugar and seasoning and allow to reduce. While the livers are simmering, fry the bread until golden brown on the outside but soft in the centre. Spread the livers on top of the croutons, sprinkle with parmesan cheese (optional) and garnish with fresh parsley.

Serve hot.

8 slices of white crusty
bread (French stick is
ideal)
Butter or oil for frying
Grated parmesan (op-
tional) and fresh chopped
parsley for garnish.

di Funghi
Mushrooms on fried croutons

Use exactly the same quantities and method as
for Crostini alla Fiorentina, but substitute fresh
mushrooms (preferably Porcini) and 1 slice of
finely chopped smoked ham for the livers and
anchovies. Serve hot.

di Pomodoro
Puréed tomatoes on fried croutons

1 oz butter
1 large clove garlic
crushed
1 pinch mixed herbs
1 14 oz tin of Italian
tomatoes
1 dessert spoon of
tomato concentrate
Black pepper
8 croutons

First prepare the tomatoes. Drain them through
a sieve discarding the juice, mash up the whole
tomatoes to a rough pulp. Fry the garlic in the
butter together with the herbs and pepper. Add
the pulped tomatoes and tomato concentrate and
bring to the boil. Let the mixture continue
bubbling for about 15 minutes to reduce. Place
the purée in the refrigerator and cool for at least
one hour. Spread on the croutons and serve
cold.

Insalata di Fagiolini
Tuscan bean salad

8 oz dried white beans*
or 1 tin of good quality
prepared white beans
3 tbs olive oil
1 tbs vinegar
Salt and black pepper
2 cloves crushed fresh
garlic
1 onion, finely sliced
1 5 oz tin of tuna fish
1 tin of anchovy fillets
Freshly chopped parsley,
large crisp lettuce and a
tomato for garnish

Mix the oil, vinegar, seasoning, garlic and onion together in a salad bowl. Add the drained beans and mix. Flake in the tuna and mix carefully. Line an unusual bowl or plate with a bed of lettuce, pile on the bean salad and sprinkle with fresh chopped parsley. Decorate with criss-crosses of anchovies and the tomato cut zig-zagged to form 2 stars.

* If using dried beans, soak overnight in plenty of cold water. Drain next day. Then put the beans in a pan full of fresh water, bring to the boil and cook for about 2-3 hours until tender.

Funghi marinati
Marinated mushrooms

1 lb fresh mushrooms

For marinade:
¼ pt white wine vinegar
8 black peppercorns
2 cloves of garlic crushed
2 fl. oz of olive oil and
2 fl. oz of water, mixed
Pinch of salt
2 bay leaves
Mixed herbs

For best results and flavour, make this recipe 1 or 2 days before it is required.

Cook the marinade in a shallow pan for 15-20 minutes, do not allow to boil. Add the whole mushrooms and simmer for 5 minutes. Leave the mushrooms in the liquid, allow to cool and then place in the refrigerator.

To serve, drain the mushrooms and place in a heavy earthenware bowl.

Italians will often serve an Insalata di Fagiolini and a Funghi Marinati as extra side dishes to accompany an Antipasto Misto or with Crostini, an idea which we can highly recommend.

Zuppa e Pasta

Stracciatella Verdi
Egg, cheese and spinach soup

4 oz cooked spinach, drained and finely chopped
1 oz freshly grated breadcrumbs
2 oz grated parmesan cheese (preferably fresh)
3 eggs
Pinch of grated nutmeg
Salt and black pepper
1 tbs chopped fresh parsley
2½-3 pts chicken stock (preferably home-made)

Beat the eggs in a mixing bowl, add the breadcrumbs, grated cheese, spinach, nutmeg, salt, pepper and parsley and about one ladle of the stock to dilute the mixture. Stir well.

Bring the remaining stock to the boil and, to this, add the egg mixture whisking continuously. Cook for about 3 minutes until the eggs float to the surface to form a feathery layer.

Serve immediately.

Zuppa Volterrana

1 oz butter or olive oil
1 14 oz tin of white kidney beans
1 aubergine, cubed
2 carrots, chopped
2 onions, chopped
1 medium potato, diced
2 large cabbage leaves, roughly chopped
1 turnip, diced
1 pinch of mixed herbs
3 cloves garlic, crushed
2 tsp, heaped, tomato purée
1 14 oz tin Italian tomatoes, mashed

A thick hearty vegetable dish which was traditionally served to the peasants working in the fields. This can either be served as an hors d'oeuvre in small dishes or ramekins, or as a main supper dish in large bowls with crusty bread. Whichever way, it is quite delicious.

Heat butter or oil in a large heavy-based saucepan, to this add the onion, garlic, salt, pepper and herbs and fry until soft. Then add the cabbage, carrots, turnip, potato and aubergine and mix well, followed by 2 heaped teaspoons of purée, and the tin of Italian tomatoes. Again mix well and then add about ½ pint or enough water just until the vegetables are nearly covered.

145

½ pt water
bread — put 4–6 slices
of a french stick into the
oven to crisp and then
crumble into largeish
bits

Cover and simmer. After 30 minutes, remove the lid and continue to cook for a further 30–40 minutes until the mixture is all soft. Add the beans and the crumbled crispy bread, mix thoroughly and simmer for a further 10 minutes. Serve piping hot.

As an hors d'oeuvres, this recipe will serve 8, as a supper dish 4.

Pasta

Home-made pasta is surprisingly easy to cook and tastes delicious. First prepare the dough — see recipes below. Next you roll the dough out into very thin sheets, sprinkle each sheet with flour to prevent sticking. (The dough quantities below will make about 4–5 sheets.) Then, depending on what dish you wish to make, follow one of the methods set out here.

Tagliatelle or Fettuccine — Flat Noodles

Roll the sheets of dough up to form swiss rolls and then cut these through into narrow slices. Un-roll and you will find that you have long flat noodles. Before cooking, either allow to dry on a floured board for 10 minutes, or wrap in foil and store in the refrigerator for up to 24 hours. (See sauce recipes, page 148.)

Lasagne — Flat Oblongs

Just use the thin rolled-out sheets, making sure that they are the size required for your baking dish. (See recipe, page 150.)

Ravioli — Pasta Parcels

If you plan to use the pasta for ravioli, make sure that you roll the dough out into 4 equal long thin oblongs. On 2 of the sheets, place the desired filling in mounds about 1½ inches apart. Brush between the mounds with water, and place a plain sheet on the top. Press down between the mounds and cut into squares. Keep on a floured teacloth until required. (See filling recipe, page 150.)

Cooking Pasta

Remember to cook all pasta in plenty of boiling, salted water with a drop of oil to prevent sticking. Home-made pasta will cook quicker than dried pasta, sometimes needing as little as 5 minutes.

Pasta Gialla
Home-made white pasta dough

1 lb plain flour
4 medium eggs
Salt

Sieve the flour including a pinch of salt, onto a board. Make a well in the centre and break the eggs into it. Work the flour into the eggs, starting from the outside, and continue kneading until the dough has become smooth, elastic and shiny.

Wrap this dough up in a warm damp cloth,* and leave to rest for half an hour, see above for pasta shapes.

(* Wet the cloth in warm water and wring out well)

Pasta Verde
Home-made green-coloured pasta dough

1 lb plain flour
4 medium eggs lightly beaten
4 oz cooked spinach, well squeezed and put through a mouli-légumes or sieve

Mix the spinach with the lightly beaten eggs and then gradually add the flour and knead to form a firm dough. See above for pasta shapes.

Pasta Rosa
Home-made red-coloured pasta dough

Use the same method and basic ingredients as for Pasta Verde, but use 2 tablespoons of concentrated tomato purée instead of the spinach.

147

Sauces

Il Ragu
Bolognese meat sauce

8 oz lean mince (of course in Tuscany this will be Vitellone)
3 oz streaky bacon, chopped
2 oz chicken livers, chopped
1 onion, chopped
1 carrot, sliced
2 sticks celery, chopped
1 7 oz tin of Italian tomatoes
¼ pt dry white wine
4 tsps tomato purée
Butter and olive oil
Salt and black pepper
1 garlic clove, crushed
Pinch of basil
1 bay leaf
1 tbs caster sugar

This traditional sauce known mostly in Italy as 'Rugu' and in England as 'Bolognese', can be used over noodles and pasta shapes or in the making of Lasagne. There are many versions of this recipe, too, but this one is, we think, fairly authentic.

Put the bacon, onion, carrot, celery, sugar, seasoning and herbs into a heavy-based pan and lightly fry in ½ oz of butter and a tablespoon of olive oil. When browned evenly, add the livers and mince. Allow to cook until all the mince is browned, tossing occasionally. Now add the wine, purée and tinned tomatoes and allow to simmer for about one hour. Adjust seasoning to taste.

Salsa alla Pizzaiola
Tomato Sauce, Neapolitan Style

1½ lbs ripe peeled tomatoes* coarsely chopped
4 cloves of crushed garlic
Salt and black pepper
oregano & basil, generous quantities to taste
3 tbs olive oil

Heat the oil with the garlic until the garlic begins to fry. Add the tomatoes, salt and pepper and herbs and cook for about 15 minutes. Do not let the sauce become a pulp.

This sauce can also be used over veal escalopes or beef steak.

(* To peel the fresh tomatoes, immerse in boiling water for a few minutes. Take out and drain. The skins will peel off easily.)

148

Pesto

2–3 cups fresh basil leaves
2 cloves garlic coarsely chopped
1 tbs of pine nuts
8 tbs of olive oil
1 oz grated parmesan
1 oz grated pecorino
Sea salt and black pepper

A Genoese sauce made from basil, garlic, cheese and pine nuts.

Blend the basil, nuts and garlic with about half the oil to form a paste. Then add the rest of the oil. Put this mixture in a mixing bowl and add the cheeses and a little seasoning.

To serve, mix into hot noodles or spaghetti.

Pappardelle alla lepre
Strips of pasta with hot hare sauce — a speciality of Tuscany

Home-made noodles
Meat from legs and saddle of one hare, cut into small cubes
3 rashers streaky bacon, diced
1 onion, chopped
1 stalk celery, chopped
2 oz butter
2 tbs olive oil
salt and pepper
3 sprigs of fresh thyme
1 tbs of plain flour
½ pt red wine
1 pt meat (beef) stock
Grated parmesan cheese when serving

Heat the butter and oil in a heavy-based sauce-pan. Fry the bacon and vegetables for a few minutes, then add the seasoning, herbs and meat, and cook until they begin to brown. Sprinkle in the flour and thoroughly mix making sure that there are no lumps. Then add the wine and stock, stirring all the time. Let the liquid reduce by about a third and then simmer (covered) over a low heat for at least 2 hours.

Cook the noodles and when drained drop them into the sauce.

Toss and serve with grated parmesan cheese.

Lasagne al Forno
Baked Lasagne

Fresh pasta, made and cooked as above, p. 146, or 8 oz of dried pasta, cooked. (Green or white pasta or a mixture may be used.)
Ragu sauce. See recipe, page 148. Double the recipe but omit the tinned tomatoes.
Béchamel sauce or sliced cheese
Butter for greasing
Grated parmesan cheese

Preheat your oven to 180°C, 350°F or gas mark 4. Grease an oblong baking dish. Place a layer of Lasagne on the bottom, followed by a layer of meat sauce and then a layer of béchamel or cheese. Repeat until the ingredients are all used, ending up with the cheese or béchamel on the top. Sprinkle with grated parmesan and bake in the oven for 30–45 minutes.

Italian housewives tend to use béchamel in preference to cheese and I certainly agree that Lasagne is best this way.

Fillings for Ravioli

Ravioli can be filled with almost anything, meat, fish or vegetables. It can be served plain, just tossed in butter and/or cheese, with a tomato sauce or with a Ragu. It is a great dish with which to experiment.

Note: Ravioli takes about 6–10 minutes cooking time to become tender.

Spinach filling

8 oz hot spinach
1 oz butter
1 beaten egg
Salt, pepper and a little grated nutmeg

Add the butter to the hot spinach and beat well. Then add the seasoning and finally the egg, mix. Place on the pasta in mounds as directed previously, see p. 147.

Salmon filling

10 oz tin of red salmon, boned, skinned and flaked
Juice of ½ lemon
Salt and black pepper
1 egg
breadcrumbs (if required)

Mix all the ingredients together to a paste, adding a few breadcrumbs if the mixture is too loose. Place on the pasta in mounds (see p. 147).

Serve tossed in butter, cream and cheese. Sprinkle with fresh chopped parsley.

Secondi Piatti

Maiale alla Toscana
Tuscan pork chops

4 lean loin pork chops
2 cloves garlic crushed
Salt, black pepper and fennel seeds
½ pt dry white wine
3 tbs olive oil

First, score the fat of the chops with a sharp knife, then season them with salt, pepper and fennel seeds.

Put the olive oil and garlic into a shallow pan, heat and allow the garlic to slightly fry. Sauté the chops in the oil until they are thoroughly cooked and browned. Add the dry white wine, cover and simmer for a further 30–40 minutes or until the chops are very tender.

Saltimbocca alla Romana
Veal wrapped in ham and sage

4 wafer thin slices of prosciutto ham
8 thin slices of veal escalope

Cut each slice of ham into two. Season the veal escalopes with a touch of salt and plenty of black pepper and put 2 sage leaves on top of each. Place a piece of ham on each and roll up and

salt and pepper
16 sage leaves (fresh)
Olive oil — about 4
tablespoons
6 fl. oz dry white wine
16 cocktail sticks

secure with a cocktail stick. Heat the oil in a sauteuse, large enough to accommodate all the parcels, fry them until cooked and browned.

Now, add the white wine, cover, and leave to simmer for about 20 minutes.

Serve two per person.

Coniglio in Salmi con funghi e olive
Rabbit cooked in wine with mushrooms and olives

4 tbs olive oil
1 rabbit jointed (about
2 lbs)
4 slices of bacon,
chopped
1 onion, chopped
1 tbs plain flour
1 tsp tomato concentrate
½ pt dry white wine
Salt and black pepper
Rosemary
2 bayleaves
1 lb mushrooms
20 black olives, stoned

Put the oil in a deep casserole, suitable for hob or oven, and heat. Fry the rabbit pieces with the onion and bacon until browned. Sprinkle with the flour, herbs and seasoning, add the tomato concentrate and the white wine. Bring to the boil, cover and simmer for 30 minutes. During the simmering slice up the mushrooms and stone the olives. Take the pan off the stove and add the mushrooms and olives, give the dish a good stir, adding extra wine or stock if necessary. Transfer the casserole to a preheated oven 230°C, 450°F or gas mark 8, and cook for a further hour or until the rabbit is tender.

Dolci

Home-made water ices

Granite, as these are called in Italian, are Italy's oldest desserts dating back to Roman times. They are both simple to make and deliciously refreshing after a heavy dinner.

If you have time to make them the same day as you wish to eat them, freeze the mixture in very shallow trays; ice-cube trays are ideal, and the 'Granite' will then only take about 3 hours in the freezer part of your refrigerator. On the other hand, they can be made a few days in advance, but the mixture will obviously become quite solid after long freezing. In this case take the trays out about 10–15 minutes before serving to soften.

To serve, flake into beautiful long stemmed glasses and top with whipped cream and flaked dark chocolate.

Granita di Limone
Lemon Water ice

1 pt water
4 oz caster sugar
½ pt strained fresh lemon juice
grated rind of one lemon

Put the sugar and water into a large pan and heat, stirring continuously until the sugar has dissolved. Bring to the boil and cook for 5 minutes.

Allow the liquid to cool and then stir in the lemon juice and rind.

Freeze in shallow trays.

Granita di Caffe
Coffee water ice

½ pt water
8 oz caster sugar
1½ pts fresh strong
black coffee

As for lemon water ice.

Granita di Frutto
Fruit water ices

8 oz caster sugar
¼ pt water
Juice of one lemon
Approximately 2 lb
fresh fruit, puréed to
produce 1 pint of pulp.
(Any fresh fruit can be
used: strawberries,
mangos, kiwi fruit . . .)

Dissolve the sugar and water over a low heat.
Bring to the boil and cook for 5 minutes. Allow
to cool. Mix in the fruit pulp and lemon juice,
stirring very well and freeze in shallow trays.

Zabaione or Zabaglione
Egg and Marsala punch

6 tbs sugar
6 egg yolks
12 tbs of dry marsala
Grated nutmeg

This mouthwatering dessert can be served hot,
warm or cold in tall glasses, and should be
accompanied by long 'cats tongue' biscuits.

Beat the egg yolks until they become frothy, then
add the sugar and continue beating until the
mixture turns to pale yellow. Dribble in the
Marsala continuously whisking until it is
thoroughly mixed in. Pour the mixture into a
double boiler and cook over almost boiling water
until the mix becomes thick and peaky. Stir, all
the time, especially around the edge of the pan
and remember never to let the water actually
fully boil or touch the top section of the pan.
When the egg punch thickens pour it into
attractive glasses and sprinkle with grated
nutmeg.

Glossary of Food Terms

Meat — Carne

lamb	agnello
beef	manzo or vitellone
veal	vitello or vitella
kid	capretto
pork	maiale
ham	prosciutto
rabbit	coniglio
hare	lepre
sausage	salsiccia
wild boar	cinghiale

Poultry — Pollame

quail	quaglia
duck	anatra
chicken	pollo
guinea fowl	faraone
turkey	tacchnio
pigeon	piccione
goose	oca

Offal — Frattaglie

liver	fegato
brains/sweetbreads	cervella
tripe	trippa
kidney	rognone

Vegetables — Verdura

garlic	aglio
carrot	carota
mushroom	fungo
cabbage	cavolo
cauliflower	cavolfiore
spinach	spinacio
beans	fagiolo
celery	sedano
turnip	rapa
onion	cipolla

155

potato	patata
peas	isello
leek	porro
pepper	peperone
artichoke	carciofo
rice	riso

Fruit — Frutta

tomato	pomodoro
peaches	pesche
apricots	albicocche
figs	fichi
apples	mela
grapes	uva
pears	pere
cherries	ciliege
strawberries	fragole
melons	melone
blackberries	more
lemon	limone
pineapple	ananas

Menu Terms

Pizza

What goes on pizzas under certain headings in Italy varies from region to region, and from one restaurant to another, but this list should help you choose.

Margherita	—	Tomato and mozzarella cheese
Napolitana	—	Tomato, anchovy, oregano and mozzarella cheese
Marinara	—	Tomato, garlic and oregano
Boscaiola	—	Tomato, mozzarella cheese and mushrooms
Campagnola	—	Tomato, mozzarella cheese, ham and mushrooms
Capricciosa	—	Tomato, cooked ham, mushrooms, artichokes and mozzarella cheese
4 Stagioni	—	Tomato, cooked ham, mushrooms, artichokes, olives and mozzarella
Siciliana	—	Tomato, anchovies, olives, garlic and capers
Pulcinella	—	Tomato, mozzarella cheese, basil and olives
Della Casa	—	of the house

Frutti di Mare — with a selection of shell-fish including octopus or squid, tomato and mozzarella cheese

Calzone — Done with fillings as above. This is turned-over pizza rather like a pie

Schiacciatina — A special bread, topped with fillings similar to those listed above

Antipasti — Hors d'oeuvres

Di Terra — Ham and salamis
Di mare misti — Mixed calamaris
Cozze e vongole — Mussels and clams
Crostini al salmone affumicato — Smoked salmon with toast
Bresaola al limone — Cured dried beef slices served with lemon
Finocchiona di fattoria — Salami flavoured with fennel seeds
Carciofi Sott'olio — Artichokes in oil

Zuppe e Pasta or Primi Piatti — Soups, pasta, rice dishes or first course

Pastina in Brodo — small pasta in clear soup
Minestrone de verdure — vegetable soup
Zuppa di fagioli — Tuscan bean soup
Spaghetti all'amatriciana — . . . with hot ham and tomato sauce
Spaghetti alla Carbonara — . . . with a sauce made from ham, eggs, oil and cream
Spaghetti Seppie Nere — . . . 'Black Spaghetti' — the sauce is made from octopus ink. Delicious, mark my words.
Penne — Pasta like small quill-shaped tubes
Penne Rustiche — . . . with garlic sausage, mushrooms and cream sauce
Cannelloni — Tubes of pasta, normally stuffed and served in a sauce
Tortellini — round shaped stuffed pasta (a bit like ravioli)
Riso or Risotto — Rice in a sauce

Secondi Piatti — Main course

¼ di Pollo al Mattone — ¼ of a roast chicken
Trippa alla Casareccia — Tripe in a tomato sauce
Faraona Arrosto — Roast Guinea fowl
Cinghiale in Salmi — Casserole of wild boar
Carni alla brace — Meat cooked over charcoal
Fettina de vitello — Slices of veal
Grigliata mista — Mixed grill

Salsiccia alla griglia	—	Italian pork sausage
Anguilla	—	Eel
Razza	—	Skate
Spigola	—	Sea bass
Sogliola	—	Sole
Gamberoni	—	Large prawns

Contorni — Vegetables

Insalata verde	—	Green salad
Insalata mista	—	Mixed salad (lettuce, tomatoes and cucumber)
Fagioli Toscani All'olio	—	White beans in olive oil
Papate Fritte	—	Chips
Spinaci al burro o all'agro	—	Spinach with butter or lemon
Peperonate	—	Red and yellow peppers in tomato sauce
Cavolini di Bruxelles	—	Brussel sprouts
Piselli	—	Peas

Formaggi — Cheese

Dolci — Dessert

Baba al Liquore	—	Small rum baba
Zuccotto	—	Ice-cream and sponge
Tartufo	—	An ice-cream chocolate truffle
Coppa gelato misto	—	Mixed ice-cream
Torte varie	—	A selection of cakes
Tiramisu	—	Sponge and liqueur base with a creamy top
Frutta	—	Fresh fruit

Miscellaneous

Coperto	—	Cover Charge
Servizio	—	Service Charge

Selected Bibliography

Gombrich, E.H. *The Story of Art* Phaidon, London, 1950
Vasari, G. *Lives of the Artists* (trs.) Penguin Classics, London, 1967
Walker, D.S. *A Geography of Italy* Methuen, London, 1967

Geographical Index

Index of Recipes

Antipasti
Antipasto misto con fichi o melone 142
Crostini alla Fiorentina 142
Crostini di Funghi 143
Crostini di Pomodoro 143
Insalata di Fagiolini 144

Zuppe e Pasta
Lasagne al Forno 150
Pappardelle alle Lepre 149
Pasta 146-7
Pesto 149
Il Ragu 148
Ravioli 150-51
Salsa alla Pizzaiola
Stracciatella Verdi 145
Zuppa Volterrana 145

Secondi Piatti
Coniglio in Salmi con funghi e olive 152
Maiale alla Toscana 151
Saltimbocca alla Romana 151

Dolci
Granita di Cafe 154
Granita di Frutto 154
Granita di Limone 153
Zabaione (Zabaglione) 154